Treatment of Sex Offenders

A Christian Approach to Psychotherapy

by

Dr. Theophilus A. Natter

Produced by
NEW LITE COUNSELING CENTER
HOUSTON, TEXAS

This work was previously published under the title *Treatment of Sex Offenders: A Psychotherapeutic Approach*, 2007, International University of Graduate Studies at St. Kitts and Nevis.

ISBN: 1453611886
EAN-13: 9781453611883

The author may be contacted at New Lite Counseling Center, 4625 North Freeway, Suite 115, in Houston, Texas 77022, or by telephone at 713-696-9885.

Acknowledgements

I would like to thank God for His many blessings on my life, giving me the ability to be who I am. By His grace and mercy He brought me this far. Without him I could not have accomplished this much. I thank my mother for her support and prayers for her nurturing and encouragement.

I would also like to thank my advisor at the Houston Graduate School of Theology, the faculty members, especially Dr. Nyler Tolliver. And I would like to thank Tommie Ann Hill Natter for her patience.

Enough cannot be said about all the help from my secretaries while I was pastoring and my staff at New Lite Counseling Center, who worked with me tirelessly.

I would like to thank Ms. Gladys Difor Natter, who encouraged and supported me, even at my lowest moments. She was always there to support me with her wonderful spirit. May God bless her.

Thanks to Dr. David Hawkins, who served as my mentor initially, and Dr. Tunji Jemi-Alade, who helped me finish my dissertation; also Dean Anderson, who corresponded with me from Dr. Crews's office to keep me informed as to the details of what was expected of me.

Finally, I would like to thank all the faculty members at International University for Graduate Studies, especially the dean, Dr. Crews, who was very encouraging and inspirational and kept up the motivation for the completed work. I will never forget what she did. May God bless her and her family in all endeavors.

Table of Contents

Acknowledgements iii

Table of Contents iv

List of Figures & Tables v

Preface vii

A Social Problem 1

How Big Is the Problem? 5

The Addiction Cycle 7

Unmanageability 8

The Addictive System 8

Other Addictions and Emotional Illness 10

Creating Space to Talk 11

Overcoming Fear and Shame 11

Responding to the News 15

Getting it out and Healing 15

Paths to Healing 17

Talk Therapy 17

Cognitive Approaches 16

The Responsivity Principle 19

Interplay of Principles 19

Types of Community Models 19

Elements of Successful Cognitive Programs 20

Proven Practices to Change Criminal Behavior 21

Caring for People God's Way 22

Sexual Addiction 22

Definition of Sexual Addiction 23

Treatment...25

The Role of Family...30

Needs and Sexuality 32

Core Beliefs and the Addict's World 34

Hope for a New Life...34

Sexual Addiction, Sexual Compulsivity, Sexual Impulsivity, or What? 44

Method..49

Participants 49

Interviews 50

Materials 60

Results 52

Questionnaire Data in Male Subjects 54

Discussion: What Can We Learn from this Study?....................59

Hypotheses 59

Toward a Theoretical Model 61

Treatment of Sexually Violent Predators... 68

Texas SVP Act 68

Council on Sex Offender Treatment.....................................68

In Conclusion... 71

Protecting and Saving Our Children..71

What We Are Up Against Now...72

Profiling the Sex Addict 73

References... 76

Endnotes 79

List of Figures & Tables

Figure 1 The Addictive System 9

Table 1 Most-Common Effects of Abuse 14
Table 2 Fast Facts 16
Table 3 Four Factors in Child's Development Leading to Sexual Addiction 32
Table 4 Core Belief 1 - Self-Image 37
Table 5 Core Belief 2 - Relationships.. 38
Table 6 Core Belief 3 - Needs 39
Table 7 Core Belief 4 - Sexuality 40
Table 8 Twelve Steps... 41
Table 9 Provisions for Addicts & Co-Addicts 42
Table 10 Key Steps 43
Table 11 Comparison of Sex Addicts & Controls... 54
Table 12 MSQ Scores for Depression Regulators vs. Rest & Controls 55
Table 13 MSQ Scores for Anxiety Regulators vs. Rest & Controls 55
Table 14 Comparison of Compulsive Masturbators with Rest & Controls 56
Table 15 Comparison of Paraphilics with Rest & Controls................................ 57
Table 16 Comparison of Dissoiators with Rest & Controls 58

Preface

I choose this topic as a way to show that "once a sex offender, *not* always a sex offender" is true, given the right treatment, and simply because I am working directly with a group of sex offenders of all ages, both male and female. I intend to show that sex offenders can be treated. The basic problem is not the sex offense, but the attitude and behavioral pattern behind it. Working with sex offenders, one has to look at the overall person, his or her environment, family background, and especially the events that led up to the offense. For instance, I have discovered that some 40% to 50% of offenders were abused as children or teenagers. In dealing with their own pain, they try to justify that pain by inflicting it on others. This is what is called a "thinking error."

This book will show that you can and should treat sex offenders in a different method. Social illness—namely drug or alcohol abuse—require a different focus. Sex offense requires a cognitive approach for direct behavior modification. This brings about a permanent change of attitude and character, thus changing the whole person. This is a long process, which can only be accomplished with the full cooperation of the patient in all phases of the treatment.

In attempting to change attitudes, you are dealing with core beliefs of an individual, which in most cases have been handed down by family imposed by environment. Core beliefs are not easy to change. You can not kill a tree by cutting off branches; you must go straight to the roots of that tree. Likewise, when dealing with the sex-offense issue, the root of the problem must be attacked. Unfortunately, most treatment providers try to deal directly with the incident offense and never address the real problem.

I became interested in working with sex offenders after looking at various issues that affect the family, for even before I was a sex-offender counselor, I was a marriage and family counselor. Therapists in any cases do not pay enough attention to the actual problem in the family, but rather focus on general issues. Also, as a preacher I have the privilege of dealing with families undergoing different dynamics. This prompted my interest in dealing with these various issues in treatment that affect families and individuals, as well as the community as a whole.

This became a challenge and very interesting for me to deal with. As I worked on my research, I became more interested into looking further into the treatment of sex offenders and their issues.

My intention is to put the family back together as a cohesive unit, rather than leaving the family no more than a fractured and pain-filled group of people under the same roof.

Theophilus A. Natter

Treatment of Sex Offenders

A Christian Approach to Psychotherapy

A Social Problem

In addressing the treatment of sex offenders and their spouses, one must carefully look into the various aspects of the couple as individuals and their families of origin and their backgrounds. Sex offense to my estimation could be classified as a social illness, which has a common bond with drug and alcohol abuse. Why do I classify it that way? Because in most cases, sexual offenses occur in the family, and in some instances there are a lot more situations going on in that family. I believe the majority of sex offenders have been sexually, physically, or mentally abused in some way at some time in their lives. Actually, sexual, drug, or alcohol abuses are not the primary problem with the offender/abuser; the primary problem is attitude/behavior.

To overcome the illness of sexual, drug, or alcohol abuse, one has to address the attitude/behavior and lifestyle issues, which may include
- ✓ taking things for granted
- ✓ disregarding what others have to say
- ✓ overlooking the seriousness of consequences of their actions.

As professionals or as society, we must start looking at why these issues are becoming so outrageous and more out of control every day.

Most parents today spend much less time with their children than parent of a few generations back. Yet in today's society, we find it ever more disturbing to leave our young people home alone without a caretaker for fear of abuse. And what is the church doing to address these social issues? What part is the church playing in dealing with these social illnesses? How seriously are parents taking these problems? And what is going on in our families today?

Moral standards today are so extremely low that as such, we have no regard for those standards, and the individual self-esteem is even less important. Sex is being promoted in every aspect of our daily dealings. Young people are exposed to sexual acts at home on TV and in the movies. It is imperative as a nation, society, and family that we start looking for a solution in dealing with these issues. Children as young as five are exposed to sex. Use of bad or sexual language is quite common. Where are we going as a people?

I do strongly believe that we need to return to the basics, where children respect parents and are taught to respect themselves and others and to fear God. This is why I believe that the church should play a great part in helping to teach our young men and women self-respect, respect for others, as well as to fear and respect God. I suggest that education and treatment are the solutions to the illness of sexual abuse, rather than confinement in prison for a short or long sentence. Sending the offender to jail only "stores" the real problem for a few years: it does nothing to change the thinking of the offender. Families should start teaching moral standards early (the golden rule), teaching their children how to talk to them when they have a problem, no matter how bad it seems. In my estimation there is a solution in dealing with the issue of sex offense. One has to look at the following areas:

1) family of origin
2) family background
3) family education
4) environment
5) lifestyle
6) belief system

The primary gateway to sexual offense is either drugs, alcohol, or both. When mind-altering substances are involved, it will initially lead to criminal activities. Sexual abuse is a very serious offense, since it is connected to emotional abuse. Sexual abuse has no barrier; it is not limited to one race or class of people. It is quite difficult to classify someone as a "sex addict' simply because of the shame associated with the illness. It keeps a lot of families or people in the shadows because of disgrace and embarrassment.

Treatment of sex offense started in the early 1970s. It became clear to the public that sex-offense crimes were occurring at alarming rates. How do we deal with sex offenders? The sex offender:

1) is put on trial
2) is probably convicted
3) is then sentenced to prison (five years to life)
4) is separated from his family and probably divorced from his wife
5) is alienated from society in general
6) reoffends upon release
7) is put away for life (either in a correctional facility or a mental institution)

The results of this program to date have been: growing prison population, costing up to $35,000 a year per inmate (this money taken from the same general fund we use to educate our children) and a growing national database of nearly half a million people, some as young as fourteen year of age, who will be barred from over 50% of neighborhoods and most educational and religious venues in the cities in which they are required to stay under state supervision (Texas Council on Sex Offender Treatment, 2002). While under these constraints, they will find it very difficult to obtain and keep employment or a descent residence "due to nature of offense." And yet failure to do so is a violation of the parole stipulations, which are treated as a contract signed upon leaving prison. A new approach is clearly called for, as the current system is itself, quite obviously, a contributing factor in the increase in violent crime. Therefore, we need to begin:

1) educating both family and society
2) and creating more intense treatment programs to enhance growth and change in both the offender *and victim*.

Punishment, although required, must eventually end. Forgiveness is the key to success; and the success all seek is simple: No more victims!

In 1980 Dr. Patrick Carnes[i] wrote a book called *Out of the Shadows*, in which he addressed the process by which one could gain freedom from his addiction. The following are excerpts from that book well worth reading and understanding, for they represent the beginning of change toward a better life:

In order to address these much desired changes, one must answer the questions: How does addiction begin? How does such a progressive insanity occur? It begins with the delusional thought processes, which are a major factor in the addict's *belief system*. That is, addicts begin with core beliefs about themselves which affect how they perceive reality. So important is this factor—the belief system—in the addiction equation, it is a theme throughout this entire book. For now, we need only point out its role in the impaired thinking of the addict.

Each person has a belief system which is the sum of the assumptions, judgments, and myths that one holds to be true. It contains potent family messages about the person's value or worth, relationships, needs, and sexuality. Within it is a repertoire of what "opinions"—answers, solutions, methods, possibilities, and ways of behaving—are open to each of us. In short, it is a model of the world. On the basis of that model we plan and make decisions, interpret other people's actions, make meaning out of life experiences, solve problems, pattern our relationships, develop our careers, and establish priorities.

The addict's belief system contains certain core beliefs which are faulty or inaccurate, and consequently, which provide a fundamental momentum for the addictions. Generally, addicts do not perceive themselves as a worthwhile person. Nor do they believe other people would care for them or meet their needs if everything was known about them, including the addiction. Finally, they believe that sex is their most important need. Sex is what makes isolation bearable. Their core beliefs are the anchor points of their sexual addiction.

Impaired Thinking. Out of the belief system—the set of interacting faulty beliefs—come distorted views of reality. Denial leads the list of ways addicts distort reality. Addicts use many devices to deny—to themselves and others—that there is a problem. Ignoring the problem, blaming others, and minimizing the behaviors are part of the addict's defensive repertoire.. Consequences such as venereal disease, unwanted pregnancy, lost jobs, arrest, and broken relationships are either overlooked or attributed to factors other than the addiction:

Venereal disease – "A lot of people get it now."
Pregnancy – "She tricked me into it."
Arrest – "Cops had it in for me. They had no real proof."
Relationships – "Her family always had problems. She
        simply couldn't handle it."

When addicts belief in the defensive rationalizations, the result is *denial* that a specific incident or behavior is part of a total behavioral pattern. Arguments, excuses, justification, and circular reasoning abound in the addict's impaired mental processes (for example: If I don't have it every few days, the pressure builds up; I'm oversexed and have to meet my needs; What she doesn't know won't hurt; She really enjoyed, asked for it, or deserved it; It doesn't hurt anybody because…; I couldn't help it, given how she acted; No one really cares; It's my way of relaxing; Women always pretend they don't want it when they do). Whatever the *rationalization*, it further cuts the addicts off from the reality of their behavior.

Sincere delusion is the act of believing your own lies. The addicts who make a commitment to change or follow through on something are sincere in their intentions. They are as sincere as when they vow to themselves to quit. They may even experience a

4

great deal of emotion—tears of pain, expressions of tenderness, or anger when someone doesn't believe in their good intentions. However their commitment to others is no more valid than their vows to themselves. It appears to be paradoxical to be sincere about telling a lie. But it is evidence of seriously impaired thinking.

How Big Is the Problem?

Because of fear, shame, and cultural baggage, most people keep this violation to themselves, making sexual abuse one of the least reported crimes in the United States. Statistics vary widely, depending on the type of research and size of the study's sample, and even what behaviors are considered abusive. It is estimated that about 87,000 children were sexually abused in 2001, this according to the Department of Health and Human Services' National Child Abuse and Neglect Data System, which tracks confirmed cases of abuse. But chronic underreporting means that no statistics truly reflect the extent of abuse in our country. These widely quoted numbers from surveys of adults looking back on their childhoods reflect how prevalent the problem is: About one in four women and one in six men report that they were sexually abused as children or teenagers.

Using these estimates, among African-Americans, that translates 3.3 million and 1.9 million men eighteen and older have reported a history of sexual abuse. If it were considered a disease, experts would have labeled sexual abuse an epidemic long ago. And if we extrapolate that estimation to include the entire population, we would recognize over 40 million people who have been sexually abused in their lives.

Comprehensive research on sexual abuse is relatively new; major studies on the issue have been produced only in the last twenty years or so.

Abuse is debilitating. Its impact on behavior is lifelong and potentially deadly. For children abuse can stunt their psychological and emotional development. E. Sue Blume writes that abused children experience "a course of development (emotional, interpersonal, sexual) that is shared, every day, with premature sexuality, lack of safety (even terror), and deformities of many life skills. The child victim's entire view of himself/herself and the world will be clouded by the effects of his/her abuse."

Most research on sexual abuse focuses on the psychological effects. Survivors are more likely to experience depression than women who weren't abused, studies show. The longer the abuse lasts and the more violent, the more severe the problems. Many psychological problems can lead to or complicate physical problems, such as reproductive disorders. Abuse also affects women's sexual choices; survivors are more likely to engage in risky sexual behavior that leads to disease and pregnancy.

The Addiction Cycle

For sexual addicts an addictive experience progresses through a four-step cycle, which intensifies with each repetition:

1) *Preoccupation* – the trance of mood, wherein the addict's mind is completely engrossed in thoughts of sex. This mental state creates an obsessive search for sexual stimulation.
2) *Ritualization* – the addict's own special routine, which leads up to sexual behavior. The ritual intensifies the preoccupation, adding arousal and excitement.
3) *Compulsive sexual behavior* – the actual sexual act, which is the end goal of the preoccupation and ritualization. Sexual addicts are unable to control or stop this behavior.
4) *Despair* – the feeling of utter hopelessness the addict has about his behavior and his powerlessness. The pain the addict feels at the end of the cycle can be numbed or obscured by sexual preoccupation, which re-engages the addiction cycle.

Sexual addicts are hostage to their own preoccupation. Every passerby, every relationship, and every introduction to someone passes through the sexually obsessive filter. More than merely noticing sexually attractive people there is a quality of desperation that interferes with work, relaxation, and even sleep. People become objects to be scrutinized. A walk through a crowded downtown area is translated into a veritable shopping list of "possibilities."

The trance is enhanced by the sexual addict's ritualization. Professionals have often wondered why sex offenders use the same "MO" (*modus operandi* or method) each time, when it only makes apprehension easier. The answer is simple. A ritual helps the trance; like a yogi in meditation, the addict need not stop and think or disrupt his focus. The ritual itself, like preoccupation, can start the rush of excitement.

The first two phases of the addict's cycle (preoccupation and ritualization) are not always visible. The addict struggles to present an image of normalcy to the outside world. The public self is a false ego, since the addict knows the incongruity of his double life. Compulsive sexual behavior, the third phase of the cycle, however, leaves a trail, despite the protective public image.

Unmanageability

The addict is caught up in the task of keeping his secret life from affecting his public life. Even so, the consequences come: arrest, unmasked lies, disruption, unmet commitments, or attempts to explain the unexplainable. The addiction surfaces in the addict's inability to manage his or her life. For a moment, recognizes that he or she cannot continue. But the impaired mental process blurs reality with euphoric recall of sexual successes. The addict faces yet again the ultimate seduction: a unique opportunity which, of course, will be "the last time."

This unending struggle to manage two lives—normal and addictive—continues. The unmanageability takes its toll. Family and friendships are abbreviated and sacrificed. Hobbies are neglected. Finances are affected. Physical needs of other kinds are unattended. The addict's lifestyle becomes a consistent violation of his or her own values, compounding the shame. The impaired mental processes result in faulty problem-solving in all areas of the addict's life. These decisions add to further unmanageability.

One of the worst consequences of the addiction is the addict's isolation. The intensity of the double life relates directly to the distance of the addicts from their friends and family. That is, the more intensely involved in compulsive sexual life the addicts become, the more alienated they become from their parents, spouses, and children. Without those human connections, the addicts paradoxically lose touch with their own selves. The unmanageability from the addiction has run its course when there is no longer a double life. When there are no longer friends or family to protect or job to hold or pretenses to be made—even though some things are valued enough to stop—the addiction is at its most destructive and violent point. The addict's world has become totally insulated from real life.

The Addictive System

As addicts move from healthy relationships to sexual compulsion, their internal processes combine to form an addictive system. The addictive system—as with all systems—contains two subsystems which support each other. Often this support occurs in repetitive, predictable cycles.

To picture the addictive system with its subsystems, consider the human body. It is a complex system with many subsystems: the nervous system, the digestive system, etc. Clearly, when on subsystem, such as the nervous system, is upset, all the other bodily systems are affected and most adjust in some way.

The addictive system starts with a belief containing the faulty assumptions, myths, and values that support impaired thinking. The resulting delusional thought processes insulate the addiction cycle from reality. The four-phase addiction cycle (preoccupation, ritualization, sexual compulsiveness, and despair) can repeat unhindered and take over the addict's life. All the other support systems, including relationships, work, finances, and health become unmanageable. The negative consequences from the unmanageability confirm the faulty beliefs, which hold that the addict is a bad person who is unlovable. In turn, the revalidated beliefs allow further distortion of reality. Diagrammed, the addictive system looks like this:

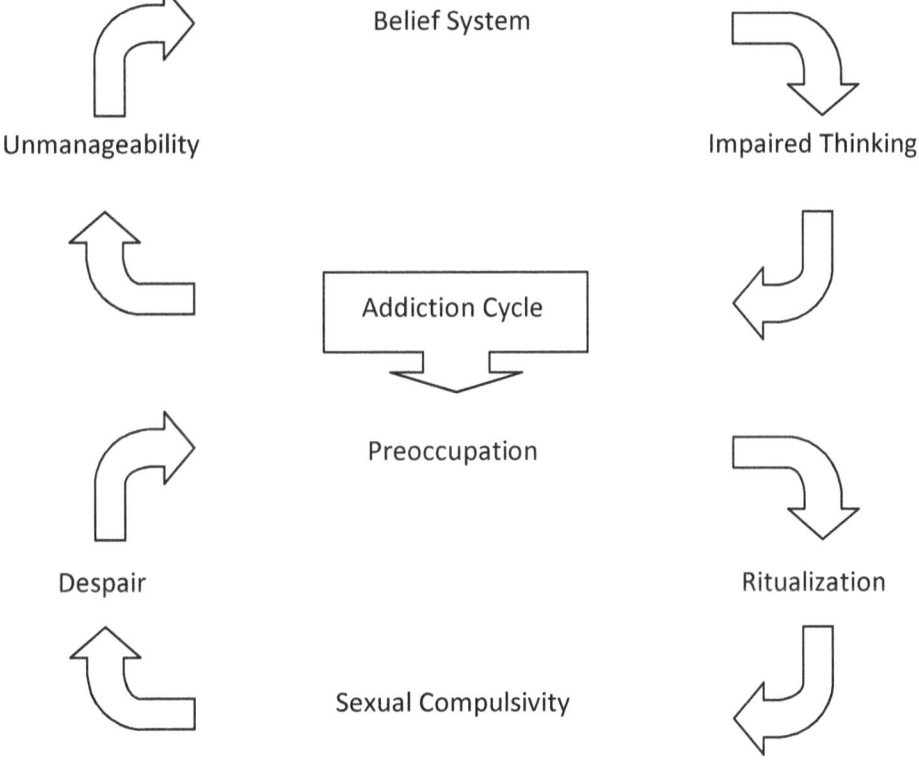

Figure 1 The Addictive System

Until the cycle is broken, it continues to feed upon itself, destroying the dreams and aspirations of the affected person.

Other Addictions and Emotional Illness

One other aspect of the addictive system is that the belief system and delusional thought patterns may support more than one addiction. Overeating, for example, is a way to minimize pain. The sexual addicts who become overweight add shame concerning their body image to their repertoire of pain. The two addictions start to reinforce each other. When the addicts believe that people are not attracted to them, their sexual addiction is partially rooted in the fear of rejection. Then they eat compulsively to kill the pain due to the fear of rejection, and as a result, put on weight. The added weight, by their standards, makes them even less desirable. Also, one way to avoid the depression after sexual binging is to binge again (with food). The two processes become interdependent. Addicts who have both addictions report that at the height of their sexual addiction, they had the greatest weight problem.

All types of compulsive behavior may be woven into the scenario of sexual addiction. Shoplifting, gambling, and spending are frequent counterparts. Physical violence is a way to release pent-up tension and is often reported as a concurrent behavior by sexually abusive families. The workaholic who gets high on the excitement of a new deal or a new breakthrough find professional life even more exhilarating when coupled with sexual addiction. In that case the sex/work addict marries the job.

Creating Space to Talk

The goal is to focus on the feelings behind the behavior, not on changing the behavior itself. Answers may not come the first time the questions are asked, but the process of asking creates a space to answer when the time is right. The following are questions to aid in this process:

- ➢ Why are you so quiet around Uncle Carl?
- ➢ You never seem to want to visit the Smiths. Why is that?
- ➢ Is there something wrong between you and your dad?
- ➢ You're angry right now. Tell me what's upsetting you.
- ➢ I know there's a beautiful body under those baggy clothes. Why do you feel you have to hide it?
- ➢ You look like you're troubled by something. Will you let me help you?
- ➢ Seems like something's weighing you down. You know, when you talk about a problem, you let it go. Let me carry it for you. I know you don't want to talk about it right now, but whenever you're ready, I'll be here to listen.

Overcoming Fear and Shame

There is a mind-body-soul connection. If emotions aren't released, they remain in the body, much like a disease. As we grow older, and the abuse becomes more distant, other reasons to keep quiet conveniently crop up. Among them are lack of time to put healing first, lack of money to pay for counseling, or obligations to family, work, and church.

Fear can be overwhelming. It can rule our lives and the lives of others in the family who might be aware of the abuse. Fear keeps us quiet and even makes us resolve to forget that we have been violated. It diminishes us, makes us timid, and makes us doubt ourselves and our place in this world. There is the fear of what people will think and what they'll say. There is the fear of retaliation and the fear you won't be believed. There is the fear that you'll jeopardize existing relationships, the fear that you'll be alone, and the fear that you actually invited the abuse. There is the fear that things will never be the same.

Most fears stem from four major ways in which abuse causes lifelong problems for survivors:

1) *Traumatic sexualization* – distress, confusion, and pain from an inappropriate sexual experience – could lead to obsessions or fears about sex.

2) *Stigmatization* – guilt, shame, and self-blame that could lead survivors to feel bad about themselves and hurt themselves or others.

3) *Betrayal* – loss of trust and grief over the loss of the relationship, especially when the abuser is related – could lead to difficulty trusting others.

4) *Powerlessness* – inability to stop the abuse – could lead to passivity or to lashing out or even to controlling behavior.

When combined with cultural expectations and our notions about our roles as children and men and women, our problems can keep us from understanding that we've been abused or keep us from admitting the horror of what really happened. Here is how fear led some people to describe their experiences:

➢ "But he didn't enter me; he only touched me." (minimizing)
➢ "It's over now." (dismissing)
➢ "I thought that's what all fathers did to their children." (rationalizing)
➢ "He was drunk; he didn't know what he was doing." (rationalizing)
➢ "I was sixteen. I felt like I should have known better." (self-blame)

One of the main factors in our survival is the strength of our families and in many cases our extended families. Unfortunately, for so many of us, our strengths have long concealed weaknesses, passed down from one generation to the next, and our survival has come at a price. The psychological toll can be likened to that of a soldier fighting a war. Though the battlefields have changed over the years, we are still in combat. Today we suffer trauma in our neighborhoods, our workplaces, and our schools. Fear can be seen in the lack of adequate housing and affordable health care, in chronic unemployment and underemployment, and in waking up each day facing the same fear.

Many of us are emotionally scarred and numb, unable to love, unable to experience our own feelings, and unable to be open and honest with one another. We've come through the fire, but we got burned. We

12

have "issues," among them anxiety, addictions, mental and physical illness, economic insecurity, limited opportunities, and an all-too-common sense of hopelessness and despair. Abuse can flourish in a family with issues.

Those family issues are like an Achilles' heel, the weak spot in our collective strength, the blind spot in our collective sight. But when we deal with our dysfunction, acknowledging and working on our weaknesses, our families can be truly strong—wholly strong—and our children valued and protected.

But no matter how severe the damage, eventually the fears must be faced, and the shame must be overcome. The secrets must be dealt with, because the silence that helps us cope in the beginning can lead to mental and physical dysfunction. Table 1 shows the most common psychological, emotional, and behavioral effects of abuse.

Table 1 Most-Common Effects of Abuse

Most-Common Effects of Abuse		
PSYCHOLOGICAL	**EMOTIONAL**	**BEHAVIORAL**
Aggression	Anger	Anxiety
Avoiding Specific Sexual Activities	Blackouts	Bullying
Concentration and Memory Problems	Confused About Sexual Orientation	Criminal Involvement
Delinquency	Depression	Difficulty Trusting Others
Eating Disorders	Emotional Clinging	Fear of Sex
Feeling Dirty	Feeling Like a Victim	Feeling Unable to Say no to Sex
Feelings of Detachment or Estrangement from Others	Feelings of Isolation and Stigma	Flashbacks/Intrusion of Thoughts
Hostility	Hyperactivity	Inability to Love or Show Affection to Children
Lack of Involvement with the Outside World	Lack of Self-Confidence	Learning Difficulties
Multiple-Personality Disorder	Need to Be in Control	Nervousness
No Interest in Sex	Phobias	Poor Self-Esteem
Post-Traumatic Stress Disorder	Problems with Interpersonal Relationships (Particularly Male-Female)	Self-Destructive Behavior
Sleep Problems	Substance Abuse	Tendency Toward Being Victimized
Thoughts of Suicide	Withdrawal	Alienation

Responding to the News

It is vital, when a survivor is finally ready to speak of his/her abuse, for the non-professional counselor to respond appropriately:

1) Listen to what he or she has to say. Find a quiet place to talk. The person may blurt out everything quickly, or he/she may yet be very hesitant. It is important to let him/her set the pace. Let person know that what he/she has to say is more important than anything else.

2) Believe him/her. Remember that one of the greatest fears of survivors is that they won't be believed or that their experience will be minimized. His or her experience will be validated by your letting him/her know that you believe him/her.

3) Ask how you can help. Tell the person that you know that he/she is in pain. Ask what he/she needs to deal with it. Ask what he/she wants to do about the abuser.

4) Encourage him/her to find outside support. Suggest calling a local crisis hotline or seeking spiritual guidance or psychological counseling.

5) Reinforce the sexual abuse was to his/her fault. Tell him or her that you're sorry that it happened and that no one had the right to do such a thing. Remind him/her that no matter what he/she did, it is the abuser who is at fault. Whatever you do, don't judge or criticize, don't blame him/her, and don't question his/her actions or express doubt about his/her account. And don't defend or make excuses for the individual he/she has accused. Don't pressure him/her to confront his/her abuser, and don't suppose what others would have done in his/her situation or compare her experience with anyone else's.

Getting it out and Healing

Like many people, you may think that therapy is not for you because you're not "crazy" or "weak." If so, consider that we all have our issues and that we can choose to do something about them, or we can choose not to. It may feel comfortable remaining where you are, if only because you are familiar with the place you're in. For some of us, changing the tune is more frightening than singing the same old song. But imagine taking on the challenge of change and composing a new score for your life. Imagine feeling entitled to joy and then going after it and grabbing hold of it. Imagine how it would feel not to be distressed, angry, bitter, anxious, or overly critical of yourself and those you love. Healing is a sense of wholeness that engulfs and overshadows even the pain of your past. With help, it is within your reach. Consider the fast facts in Table 2, originally published in 1980, realizing that the statistics have almost certainly not improved in the thirty years since.

Table 2 Fast Facts

Fast Facts
(from *No Secrets, No Lies* by Robin Stone, 1980)
36% of women with a history of childhood abuse have received a diagnosis of anxiety or depression from a physician within the past five years, compared with 14% of women without such a history.
Among women with high levels of depressive symptoms, more than one of three (37%) thought she needed to see a mental-health professional in the past year; yet only one of five (20%) actually did so.
46% of Black American women have a high level of depressive symptoms, compared with 37% of White women, 43% of Hispanic women, and 41% of Asian-American women.

Paths to Healing

No two paths to healing are the same. Your experiences and needs are far different than mine. You may be in a low-grade state of depression or you may be on the verge of suicide or you may be somewhere in between. You may find that sifting through your past to solve problems today is too tedious; you may simply want to focus on changing negative thoughts and behavior. You might prefer the camaraderie of a group to the one-on-one of individual therapy; or a holistic approach to the traditional one. You might embrace artistic forms of healing, like dance, art, or journaling, instead of or in addition to talk therapy. You might find it easier to turn to a spiritual healer you know or to a new mental-health professional from whom you have nothing to hide.

Talk Therapy

Individual Therapy: Talk therapy or psychotherapy has been a mainstay of mental-health care for the last century. It is most often used to treat problems like anxiety and depression and to help people reach specific goals. The main benefit of therapy is to begin the process of healing. It is for people not to feel isolated, to feel supported and validated, particularly in sexual-abuse cases where the family might not believe an offense has occurred. If left untreated at any given time depression can disrupt both the family and personal life of all parties involved.

Types of therapy include the analytical approach (exploring the past, the conscious and the unconscious) and the increasingly popular cognitive approach (shorter-term treatment, more like coaching to reach specific goals). Many therapists practice a combination of the two, along with other techniques that include behavioral therapy (zeroing in on behaviors that lead to depression). However, in talk therapy a client meets with a trained professional to discuss issues, concerns, and goals. The service provider can be a psychologist, a psychiatrist, a social worker, or other trained, licensed counselor. Many of us turn to members of the clergy for counseling, and if this is what you want to do, make sure the person you choose is trained to deal with issues related to sexual abuse. If the clergyman knows other family members involved, consider whether he or she may be biased.

17

Be very careful with the following statement; ethnicity has absolutely nothing to do with the real issue, but is a side issue that can block the way toward the desired goal, healing. For a host of reasons, including embarrassment and a deep mistrust of a majority of majority Caucasian medical profession, African-Americans have been slow to embrace traditional therapy. When we do, we often find ourselves sitting across from a counselor who hasn't a clue to the complexities of our culture, our history, and our challenges. He may only see our problems from the Caucasian middle-class perspective. Since the late 1960s, experts have developed multicultural approaches to therapy that incorporate the values, customs, and traditions of non-Caucasians. One of these, the African-centered approach builds upon basic tenets we have inherited from our emphasis on the collective "we" (as opposed to the individual "I") and our commitment to supporting our communities. These values can then be applied to all segments of the community without regard to the ethnic realities of life as an "unhyphenated" American.

Cognitive Approaches

There are two main types of cognitive programs: cognitive skills and cognitive restructuring. Cognitive-skills training is based on the premise that offenders have never learned the "thinking skills" required to function productively and responsibly. This skill deficit is remedied by systematic training in skills such as problem-solving, negotiation, assertiveness, anger control, and social skills focused on specific social situations, like making a complaint or asking for help.

Cognitive restructuring is based on the premise that offenders have learned destructive attitudes and thinking habits that point them to criminal behavior. Cognitive restructuring consists of identifying the specific attitudes and ways of thinking that point to criminality and systematically replacing them with positive attitudes and ways of thinking.

Cognitive restructuring and cognitive skills care complementary and can be combined into a single program. When practiced in a community model, re-socialization can be enhanced and accelerated. Both cognitive strategies take an objective and systematic approach to

18

change. Change is not coerced; offenders are taught how to think for themselves and to make their own decisions. (This is an important part of Christian training.)

Cognitive corrections programs regard clients as fully responsible for their behavior. Thinking is viewed as a type of learned behavior. Dishonesty and irresponsibility are the primary targets of change. Limit-setting and accountability do not conflict with the cognitive approach to offender change; they support it. These programs are particularly useful for substance-abusers, because acceptance of limit-setting is a primary need associated with early recovery.

The Responsivity Principle

The *responsivity principle* refers to the delivery of treatment programs in a manner that is consistent with the ability and learning style of the client. Sexual-abuse-treatment effectiveness (measured by recidivism) is influenced by the interaction between client characteristics (relative empathy, cognitive ability, maturity, etc.) and service characteristics (location, structure, skill and interest of providers, etc.). Characteristics such as gender and ethnicity of an offender also influence responsivity to treatment.

Interplay of Principles

Application of the risk principle helps identify *who should receive treatment*. The criminogenic need principle focuses on *what should be treated*. The responsivity principle underscores the importance of *how treatment should be delivered*.

Types of Community Models

Community models can take many shapes and designs. The most-familiar interpretation of the community model is the therapeutic community or TC. The TC has shown success with the most-severely drug-abusing and criminogenic offenders. TCs have also been used successfully in modified forms to help develop pro-social behavior among other special-needs populations, such as sex offenders, mentally ill offenders, and dually diagnosed offenders. There is some evidence that offenders who are more pro-socially oriented (low-risk offenders) do not require the highly structured, long-term, and expensive TC modality. Although modified TC models are sometimes employed with low-risk offender populations, successful correction programs treat low-risk offenders separately.

Elements of Successful Cognitive Programs

Cognitive programs operate with the following assumptions:
1) Cognitive learning is the key to social behavior. Problem behavior is almost always rooted in modes of thinking that promote and support that behavior. Permanent change in problem behavior demands change at a cognitive level (change in the underlying beliefs, attitudes, and ways of thinking).
2) Authority and control that increases or intensifies resentment and antisocial attitudes is counterproductive. Punitive methods of controlling behavior all too often reinforce modes of thinking that were responsible for the initial antisocial behavior. The alternative to punitive measures is not permissiveness, but rather a rational strategy of authority and control combined with programs of rational change, which give hope instead of fear.
3) Authority and control can achieve both compliance and cooperation. Authority can define rules and enforce consequences, which remind and encourage clients to make their own decisions. AS clients learn to make conscious and deliberate decisions, they accept responsibility for their behavior and can take back the control of their own lives with a new authority gained through education.

Proven Practices to Change Criminal Behavior

Pro-social thinking can be taught. Programs of cognitive change can teach pro-social ways of thinking, even to severely criminogenic and violent clients. The effectiveness of cognitive programs in changing antisocial behavior has been demonstrated by practical application over time.

The value of cognitive strategies extends well beyond the correctional environment. Cognitive principles can be applied to victim restitution, educational settings, personal development, and as an overall approach to public safety through offender change.

Essential to any integrated approach is the inclusion of relapse prevention strategies that typically incorporate the following elements:

1) Development of and rehearsal of an individualized alternative pro-social response specific to the behaviors and/or circumstances that increase the risk of re-offending for the person in question.
2) Development of self-monitoring skills and the ability to anticipate problem situations
3) Training of significant others, such as family, friends, and employers (who are willing to learn how to recognize triggers and risk situations) to reinforce pro-social behavior

Caring for People God's Way

To realize how sexually saturated our culture is, simply remember what the availability of pornography was in the 1950s when Hugh Hefner published the first issue of *Playboy* (just as a starting point, not in judgment) and what it is today with the largely unregulated Internet. Now add to that the sexual stimulus that hits you on a daily basis as you watch TV, read a magazine, listen to the radio, go to a movie, or visit a shopping mall. You might even think about sex when you go to church and notice what the young girls in our youth groups are wearing.

Christianity Today, through its Leadership Journal, discovered in a survey of pastors that 40% of evangelical pastors admitted to looking at Internet pornography. One third of those said that they had looked at it in the last year. There is a moral crisis in Christian leadership, and rarely a day goes by when we don't hear of some pastor or leader who has fallen. But Satan has been attacking great church leaders since the beginning of time. Think of Samson, who visited a prostitute in Gaza and had perhaps a love addiction with Delilah. Then there was King David, who had an affair with Bathsheba and committed murder to cover it up. And what of Solomon, whose 700 wives and 300 concubines turned him away from the true worship of God.

Sexual Addiction

If ever there was a time to understand how sexual sin can become addictive, it is now. Paul's time was not much different when he said in Romans 12:2, "Don't be conformed to the way of the world." Roman culture was also saturated with sex. What is even more frightening today is how available sex is electronically on the Internet. Pornography is the number one selling product. People who might otherwise feel inhibited are taking advantage of the relative privacy of the Internet to view levels of pornography that used to be available only in the darkest places. Prostitutes now have their own websites. Matching services can find you a sex partner in less than 24 hours.

Our churches are being attacked by the moral failure of their members and leaders alike. It is time for Christian counselors to get the knowledge they need to be able to identify and treat this terrible disease.

"It has been demonstrated that you can also control sexual behavior with intense cognitive therapy in a long-term treatment program. The program must stress positive self-awareness, empathy, and a real concern for the feelings and needs of others before self. However, if the program only serves to remind the patient of past behavior, the past behavior will, in most cases, remain a current pattern of thinking; it is the pattern of thinking that must change in the patient if the behavior is be changed. Continued and intense reminders of past behavior will become toxic to the improvement of this psychiatric condition and can become a catalyst for further criminal-thinking patterns, starting the offense cycle over again, with the same result." (Laaser, 1992, 1996, 2002)

Definition of Sexual Addiction

The five classic criteria that define sexual addiction are unmanageability, the feeling avoidance, emotional, relational, and physical factors.

Unmanageability: A sex addict believes that his/her problems with sex are out of control and that he/she is powerless. They have tried to stop and can't. Prayed and besought God to remove their lust. Many have sought salvation in different churches and denominations. What is true is that sex addicts hang onto wanting to control their lives. They are participants in original sin, the inability to *trust God.* Sex addicts are "double-minded." (James 1:8) A part of them wants to get well and a part of them doesn't. Sex has been the way they seek love for most of their lives. They may be Christian, but they want God to magically cure them without work on their part. Unmanageability starts with fantasy or preoccupation with sexual thoughts at the top of the cycle. What is actually unmanageable is the fact that they haven't totally surrendered to God.

Feeling Avoidance: Do not equate sexual sin with sexual addiction. There are many who sin sexually, but do not become involved in repetitive, progressive, and unmanageable behaviors. Addicts are lovely, angry, and anxious. They need to deal with those negative feelings by ignoring them or by disconnecting from them. The consequences of immoral sexual activity have historically and will always lead to negative consequences.

Emotional Factors: Sex addicts are emotionally wounded. In a study already cited Dr. Patrick Carnes found that 81% of sex addicts had themselves been sexually abused; 74% physically abused; and 97% emotionally abused. Further research is needed to see if the same kinds of abuse statistics apply to the legions of men and women who are becoming addicted to the Internet.

"Abuse leaves addicts lonely, angry, frightened, and confused. They develop core beliefs: 'I am a bad and worthless person. No one will love me as I am. No one will take care of me but me. Sex is my most-important need.' At some time in the life of an addict, sex becomes a solution to those feelings. When it does, it gets 'cemented' into the brain as the way out or escape from the feelings. This is referred to as the 'arousal template.' This could be a cause-and-effect response involving the 'fight-or-flight' tendencies in the individual. (Laaser, 1992, 1996, 2004)

Relational Factors: Abuse can lead to relational and intimacy difficulties. They long for approval and usually develop approval disorders, which many have called "co-dependency." If a child does not learn healthy connections, how will he know about them as an adult? Lately attachment theory has begun to explain how devastating this can be. Addicts suffer from an intimacy disorder. They feel that if they were really known, people would hate them and leave them. This pre-disposes them to lying and avoiding the truth.

Addicts hope that their relationships, especially their marriages, will solve all these attachment and intimacy issues. When they don't seem to, at least in the magical way addicts would like, they get angry with themselves and others. They may think that they have found the wrong spouse or friends. As they take this feeling further, it may lead them to think that they need and even deserve to find a better relationship. Obviously, this can lead to affairs and other unhealthy relationships. Their co-dependency can keep them locked into these relationships and they wind up feeling trapped. The bottom line etiologically is that sex addicts may feel that the only way they get their needs for love and nurturing is through sex and/or infatuated romance.

Physical Factors: Addicts become neuro-chemically tolerant to the chemicals that sex, love, and romance produce. They are literally physically dependent. When sex is combined with excitement and danger, adrenaline can be dependently involved. It is very common for sex addicts to be addicted to other substances or activities that produce these same chemicals. For example, Dr. Patrick Carnes[i] found that roughly 50% of sex addicts are also alcoholics. In the same study, Dr. Carnes found that the more severe the abuse was to the addict as a child, the more likely they are to have multiple addictions.

Many researchers believe that there is a correlation between attention deficit disorder (ADD or ADHD) and addiction. One belief is that untreated ADD will "metastasize" to addiction. Suffering from ADD can also mean that a person is simply bored and craves stimulation in whatever way he can get it.

Treatment

Emotional: Since sex addicts are profoundly abused, treating trauma wounds will be one major goal of treatment. The treatment of trauma usually consists of using various counseling methods to identify the history of trauma and allowing the person to express and understand feelings about his or her history. Learning how people have coped with trauma is vital. Using sex as a coping strategy is one of the ways to "numb" the pain of their trauma.

Shame is the by-product of trauma, and spiritual truth is an essential part of the treatment of trauma. Reminding addicts that they are "fearfully and wonderfully made" (Psalms 139) and that Christ died for them is vital.

Grieving the loss of so much love and nurture is often a part of the process of healing from trauma. I have found that the only way to truly heal trauma is to help addicts find meaning in it. Addicts can spend lots of time being victims and feeling sorry for themselves, or they can ask, "What meaning can I make of this?" It is true that God can work for good in any situation. (Romans 8:28) God can use our experience of trauma to make us stronger and more sensitive to others. It can also be true that when we experience the pain of our trauma, we are experiencing the pain of all humanity.

Addicts can learn that they grow together in community when they share their pain with others who also have pain. I believe that is what Jesus asks us to do when he says in Matthew 11:28-30 that we can find comfort in our weariness when we take upon ourselves his yoke. When we know that Jesus shares our pain through the cross and that thereby he takes it upon himself, it becomes a whole lot lighter and easier burden to

25

bear.

The final act of healing from trauma is to forgive those who have "persecuted" us. That is clearly our spiritual calling. Addicts must come to know that when they carry the burden of anger and resentment, it leads to despair.

Most treatment for addiction would seek to help addicts stop fantasizing about sex. Some would have them "take every thought captive" by just avoiding the thoughts or by guarding the mind against them. I have found that it is better to ask what the fantasies are trying to teach us about the pain. I believe that every fantasy is an attempt to heal a wound from the past. In the fantasy a person will create ways to stop the memory of harm or ways to get the love and nurturing that was missing earlier in life.

Relational: Sex addicts will need how to connect intimately. That is why the honesty of support groups can be a vital part of treatment. Just as others may not trust addicts, addicts don't trust that they can be honest without others without further attack. (Self-Preservation)

In order to build trust, addicts will have to be completely sober and completely honest about their thoughts and behaviors. That is why I believe it is vital for an addict to disclose his or her story to spouse, offspring, and close friends of the family. This can be daunting. The actual specifics of the story are not as important as the exact nature of the activity. It is morally imperative to do so, particularly if the addict has put others in physical danger (such as through exposure to disease).

First, each spouse must surrender to Christ. Second, each spouse must surrender the other to Christ, accepting that they cannot control each other. Third, the couple must surrender their marriage to Christ. Only in this act of "one flesh union" can couples build a better relationship.

Couple therapy for sex addiction will involve three equal pieces of work: the addict, the spouse, and the couple. Couples' counseling from day one is vital in facilitating growth. Today there are workbooks to help people on the journey.

Physical: Because sex addicts have become neuro-chemically tolerant to sex, they will need to go through a period of total abstinence from sexual expression in any form. They should sign a contract not to be "sexual with themselves or others." However, this contract can in no way be coerced, or it becomes invalid and useless. This would include spouses. It is important to help spouses understand the need for this and to agree to it of their own free will. Paul said in I Corinthians 7 that couples "should not deprive each other except by mutual consent and for a time so that they may devote themselves to prayer." (vs. 5) When addicts do this, they will detoxify their brains and may go through similar, albeit less severe, symptoms as an alcoholic would. It is important during this time to find them real support.

After about 7-14 days of abstinence, addicts will notice that it becomes easier to stay free of sexual acting out. My experience would suggest that it is easier to be completely abstinent than regularly sexual with a spouse. This is a neuro-chemical phenomenon. Single people, therefore, may have an easier time being sober than married people. For an addict, there is no amount of sex that is ever enough to satisfy biological desire. They will always want more. I have found that the only way to satisfy sexual desire ultimately is in the spiritual intimacy of marriage. Within the bonds of matrimony are the most intimate moments when two people do indeed become one. The couple plan and start a family together; children are reared and become adults, who copy the behaviors of the parents. Where the marriage is respected and nurtured, the children grow to respect the institution of marriage and value the family relationship and then pass those value systems along to the next generation. Anything else nearly always ends with more suffering and depression, which only serves to start the addiction cycle again.

Addicts may need to have physical evaluation for the possibility of STDs. They may also need help with any sexual dysfunction that may have developed. Getting competent Christian sex therapy could be an important step. Physical self-care is also vital. Lack of exercise, proper nutrition, and adequate rest could make addicts more vulnerable to temptation.

Finally, psychiatric treatment for any imbalance of neuro-chemistry is incredibly important. Since ADD/HD may be a co-morbid condition, treatment for it could often be the missing link in staying sober. Brain scan imaging can be indicated, especially in those cases where traditional psychiatry does not seem to be able to adequately diagnose the problem.[ii]

Cognitive/behavioral: Talk therapy and spiritual direction will be essential parts of a treatment plan. Helping addicts understand their own wounded core beliefs and the truth of the gospel will be a life journey of healing.

Helping addicts find and maintain accountability is a critical part of treatment. The book of Nehemiah is a virtual blueprint of how to do this. First, accountability begins with willingness and brokenness. Second, accountability requires confession and a spirit of repentance. (Neh. 1) Third, accountability is maintained in groups of men or of women dedicated to sexual purity. These are the "warriors" of an addict's life. (Neh. 2:9) Also, the addicts must get rid of all the "dung" in their lives (Neh. 3:14), meaning pornography, affairs, secret phone numbers, and irrational thinking. The addicts must identify the enemy in order to discover how they become vulnerable in their rituals. Addicts must prepare when they are strong for the temptations that will come, and they must not wait until it happens, for that is part of the temptation. Addicts must be accountable to do positive actions and defend against negative ones. Addicts must find a higher calling or purpose for which to recover, such as fighting for their families and their homes. (Neh. 4:14) Addicts must learn how to define their sobriety and the rituals that lead them into acting out. For most Christian addicts, sobriety will mean no acting out with self (masturbation) and others outside of marriage. Masturbation has sometimes been controversial in the Christian community, especially with singles. My experience is that masturbation could be looked at as a positive or a negative activity or habit, depending upon frequency and emotional state of the addict.[iii]

Finding sobriety from sex addiction is in some ways more like an eating disorder than it is like alcoholism. Both sex and eating are natural desires of the body. Just as eating can't be totally abstained from, so sex (for those married) can't be given up either. Learning how to be sexual or to eat for the healthy purposes of it is vital to the journey of accountability.

Spiritual: Sex addicts will need to answer three spiritual questions in order to begin the journey of healing:

1) *"Do you want to get well?"* is the question Jesus asked the paralyzed man in John 5:6. Instead of being physically paralyzed, this man may have adopted an attitude of being paralyzed. Addicts have adopted the attitude of being addicts. Before any change can begin, anyone seeking change must be willing to give up his or her own control and give it to God. As it was with the man facing Jesus, it had to be his choice alone. This choice can in no way be forced, coerced, or caused to happen. It must come from the heart of the person in need.

2) *"What are you thirsty for?"* In the story of the Samaritan woman in John 4, Jesus tells her that earthly water does not satisfy thirst and that only "living water" does. Recovering sex addicts know that they have been thirsty for sexual solutions that only resulted in pain and suffering for themselves and their families. That thirst must be refocused toward Christ. All else will fade to insignificance in comparison. The "living water" solves the problem when that water is accepted.

3) *"Are you willing to die to yourself?"* In John 11, when Jesus heals Lazarus, he is demonstrating that he will let someone die in order for them to experience the resurrecting power of a relationship with him. Addicts are often like Lazarus's two sisters, Mary and Martha, and think that if Jesus would only have come, he wouldn't have died. Only addicts who stop looking for magic answers and are willing to die to their own control and power will find true healing. Death is not going to be avoided. But for those who have "died to Christ," death is no longer a fear, but merely a turn on the road of changing reality.

Addicts must have a vision of God's calling in their lives. They have created fantasies of their solutions and must now find God's solution. Addicts without a vision will perish. A vision is the motivation to follow God and not the self (like a dog chasing its tail). Fantasy is a magic answer; vision is God's. Vision directs all we do and gives us an appetite and a thirst for "things above" and not "things below." When addicts start a cycle of vision (looking up to Christ), it will lead to healthy discipline, healthy behavior, and joy. This is opposed to the addict's historical cycle of fantasy, ritual, acting out, and despair.

Recovery from addiction is the reversal of the alienation that is integral to the addiction. Addicts must establish roots in caring communities. With that support, addicts can stay straight as they struggle for a perspective on their lives. With help addicts can integrate new beliefs and discard dysfunctional thinking. Without the mood-altering insanity to insulate them from the knowledge about their own selves, they become participants in the restoration of their own sanity in a new and stable lifestyle.

All forms of addiction are vicious because they further the inability to trust others. Yet without help from others, the addict cannot regain control, for the addiction feeds itself. Sexual addiction is especially virulent, because few forms of fixation or excitement are as supercharged with social judgment, ridicule, and fear. Consequently, seeking help is especially difficult for sexual addicts.

One of the proven paths to recovery is the Twelve Steps of Alcoholics Anonymous. This book proposes the Twelve Steps as a way for sexual addicts to emerge from their double lives. Across the country local groups have modified the Twelve Steps for the sexually compulsive.

The Twelve Step Program helps members restore the living network of human relationships, especially in their family. The Program asks the addicts first to accept their addiction by looking at their addiction cycle and its consequences, i.e. to admit that they are powerless over their sexual behavior and their lives have become unmanageable. With that admission, the members then are able to start the rebuilding of relationships by taking responsibility for what they have done and making amends where possible.

The Role of Family

Sexual addiction, as a family illness, parallels almost every other emotional and addictive disorder. For the past twenty years professionals in many disciplines have been documenting the family as a system regulated by rules and roles, understanding and misunderstanding. The family system has the capacity to sustain unity, establish distance between family members, allow individual uniqueness, and produce organized effort. The family, above all, has a range of options available to maintain balance. Being balanced for family members makes them feel normal. Not always, but sometimes that means keeping things the same, even if they are painful.

Suicide, schizophrenia, alcoholism, runaways all are part of the family epic. For example, in alcoholism, treatment of the spouse alone has been shown to promote recovery in the alcoholic. Now, throughout the ranks of specialists in addiction, treating the entire family is regarded as critical. It is recognized that the more family members are involved, the higher the recovery rate. Moreover, spouses, parents, and children, by virtue of their participation in the family insanity, have a right to recovery for themselves.

Whatever the disorder, family members are often unaware of their own pain. They very clearly do not understand their condition in the family drama. A sign of the family member's delusion is his or her deep-seated conviction that they had little to do with it. If only that other person:

➢ would stop drinking,
➢ could control his or her eating,
➢ could keep his or her feet on the ground,
➢ had not run away,
➢ was not so obsessed with sex,
➢ could manage life better,
➢ were more responsible,
➢ could keep a job, or
➢ would grow up and stop acting like a child.

A more-severe delusion is when the family does not even acknowledge that there is a problem.

Needs and Sexuality

There are four perceptual factors in a child's development which ultimately become part of the sexual addiction and are illustrated in Table 3. These perceptions form themselves into the core beliefs central to the addictive system. They are conclusions that will govern the choices and behaviors during the child's adult life.

Addicts report that as children they felt desperately lonely, lost, and unprotected. Not only was there a lack of nurturing, but there was no one to show them how to take care of themselves or keep them from harm. Not being able to count on—depend on—the adults in one's life to meet needs is a key element in addictions. As the child matures, there begins a search for that which is dependable, something that can be trusted to make him/her feel better. Trust and dependency are the issues that determine personal strength and confidence or vulnerability and enslaving addiction. In the lonely search for something or someone to depend upon—which has already excluded parents—a child can start to find those things that always comfort, always feel good, always are there, and always do what they promise. For some, alcohol and drugs are the answer; for others it is food; and for yet others it is sex, which usually costs nothing and nobody can regulate.

Table 3 Four Factors in Child's Development Leading to Sexual Addiction

Four Factors in a Child's Development Leading to Sexual Addiction (Perceptions = Core Beliefs)	
Self-Image	How Children Perceive Themselves
Relationships	How Children Perceive their Relationships with Others
Needs	How Children Perceive their own Needs
Sexuality	How Children Perceive their own Sexual Feelings and Needs

This choice stems from the addict's third core belief, which is about needs: *My needs are never going to be met if I have to depend upon others.* In healthy families, children have a deep sense that their parents care for them, as opposed to abandoning them.

Healthy parenting includes touching, loving, affirming, and

guiding. The child feels cared for even when struggling with rules and limits. Trust on one's self as well as trust in others emerges in that relationship.

When a child's exploration of sexuality goes beyond discovery to routine self-comforting because of lack of human care, there is opportunity for addiction. Sex becomes confused and comforting and nurturing. The assumption is made that everyone else feels and acts the same. Therefore, to feel secure means to be sexual.

Consequently, the child's relationships with people have the potential of being replaced with an addictive relationship with sexuality. Addiction is a relationship, a pathological relationship in which sexual obsession replaces people. And it can start very early. The final core belief of the addict emerges clearly: *Sex is my most-important need.*

The kinds of childhood situations described are further complicated when the children are surrounded by negative rules, messages, and judgments about sex. When addicts and spouses study their families of origin, they are flooded with memories of events where they were told that being sexual was bad, or worse, that they were bad for being sexual.

When children's primary source of comfort is sex, and yet they are told by those whose judgments count the most that to be sexual is perverse, the conclusion they make about themselves are clear. They are unlikeable. They need to hide that central part of themselves, which others will despise. Rather than repressing sexual behaviors, they hide them or keep them secret. Needing to keep that central part of themselves secret adds to the pain and loneliness, which in turn creates need for comfort, making the need for the sexual fix that much more necessary.

The fusion between sex and nurturing is cemented if the child is a victim of sexual abuse. Level 2 and level 3 addicts are almost always sexually abused as children. Parents, clergy, older siblings, relatives, physicians, friends, teachers, babysitters: a wide range of people have opportunities to exploit a child. Children learn from the important adults in their lives how to have a significant human relationship. Once a person has learned how to have a relationship with other people, then the sexual component can be added as a special expression of a special relationship. If parents or significant adults are sexual with a child, the young person will always have difficulty sorting out sexuality and relationship.

Core Beliefs and the Addict's World

All addicts can find elements of their sexual compulsiveness in their early years. The core beliefs that were part and parcel of the addict's growing up become central to the addict's world as an adult. Each core belief contributes to the disconnection between the interior world and the addict experiences with its pain and shame.

> "...because this sample was very small and we performed only limited assessment of the childhood factors, these results cannot be regarded as definitive."

> "...predisposition to use substances or behaviors o alleviate emotional pain may an "intimacy dysfunction," which could result from child sexual abuse or neglect."

> "...man in monogamous relationships had lower MSQ scores."
> (Carnes, 1983)

Hope for a New Life

The core beliefs that lead to study of the Bible will guide anyone toward a better life. But that life is closed to any person who chooses to ignore or refuses the teachings in the Bible. For that person, the above quotes are offered as a possible result, without hope for change. With God all things are possible. And all things, including new life, can indeed be realized.

As one of my colleagues recently put it, "In our current sexually absorbed culture, working with sex addicts is a growth industry." (Laaser, 1992, 1996, 2004) There is no shortage of work to go around. I encourage you to be involved if you feel capable. There are plenty of ways to acquire further training and even to get certification. AACC conferences and video series are a great source.

There is one last word of caution. Working with sex addicts will challenge a counselor's own sexuality. Listening to the stories can be troubling at some times sexually provocative at others. If a counselor's own sexual health is not in good order, then working with addicts can be dangerous. When in doubt, refer to a competent therapist in your area.

When successful work with sex addicts and their spouses is accomplished, however, the transformation of lives and marriages is a very fulfilling result.

In my research for this paper, I found myself online one evening in conversation with an Imam in Mecca. He made the following quote on the topic of sexual abuse: "God made woman from man's rib, not from his feet to be walked on by him, nor from his head to top him, nor from under his arm to be protected by him, by his side to be his partner in life and from his heart to be loved by him." (Surah 313 the Holy Quran)

22 آدَمَ إلى أحضَرَهَا امرْأةُ الضّلع هَذِهِ مِنْ وَعَمِلَ.

23 آدَمُ فقالَ: «أُخِذَتْ امرْيءٍ مِن لأنّهَا امرْأةٌ تُدعَى فهيَ. لحمِي مِنْ ولَحْمٌ عِظامِي مِنْ عَظْمٌ الآنَ هَذِهِ».

24 لِهَذا، فإنْ الرّجُلَ يَترُكُ أباهُ مُعُوّا وَيَلْتَصِقُ بامرْأتِهِ، وَيَصيرانِ جَسَداً وَاحِداً.

25 وكانَ آدَمُ وَامرْأتُهُ، عُريانَيْنِ وَلَمْ يَعْتَرِهُمَا الخَجَلُ.

The King James Bible puts it this way:
> [22]And the rib or part of his side which the Lord God had taken from the man He built up and made into a woman, and he brought her to the man. [23]Then Adam said, This [creature] is now bone of my bones and flesh of my flesh; she shall be called Woman, because she was taken out of man. [24]Therefore a man shall leave his father and his mother and shall become united and cleave to his wife, and they shall become one flesh. [25]And the man and his wife were both naked and were not embarrassed or ashamed in each other's presence.

If you consider the way women are treated in this modern age, the above stated philosophy becomes rather strange, bordering on the bizarre. Women and sexuality are marketed like any other consumable item, not as possible partners for life, not as companions for sons of Islam, not as mates with whom Christian sons might become one flesh, but merely as a motivator by which cosmetics, clothing, and many other products are sold in order to enhance the chances for sexual contact. You can find examples on the magazine rack in many Christian-owned and Islamic-owned convenience stores examples of this. No longer looked upon as wonders created in God's image, young women (and men) are nothing more than objects of lust and desire of the basest type or as tools to be used to manipulate the public. Is this God's way? More importantly, are we looking to God for guidance in life?

I am Christian. I know what is to turn away from God. It hurts! But the wonder of it all is that when you finally tire of all the pain and turn around again, guess Who is and always will be right there. Christianity has suffered through many years of error (the Crusades, the Inquisition, the witch hunts, and countless wars) created by false teachings of mortal men claiming divine guidance. The politically ambitious have long used misinterpretation of Scripture to build their power base, only to offer the blood of those being governed as justification of the false teachings. Has anyone learned anything from all the bloodshed?

In any death of any person of any religion, God takes no pleasure. But His joy when only one person turns back to worship Him is boundless. Do not be fooled. He was and is and always will be the one true God and will judge us all on the same day. I prefer to face that judgment day with Jesus Christ as my lawyer, not alone, facing the balance scales, knowing full well how many times in my life I've sinned by thought or deed.

When anyone treats a woman (or a man) badly, the Creator is offended. His act of creation made all of us possible. His was the perfect plan to build the human race from a single seed of thought, spoken and made man. We all too often lose sight of that truth in order to pursue our own desires and lusts, much to our loss and shame.

In the "modern age of information," we have built massive databases to keep up with all the people who have offended *our* laws. This could be rightfully so. But at what cost? Do any people placed on the list deserve a second chance at life? Or should the all be shoved aside in every way possible? Is there a chance they might rediscover the truth in life? It is certain that we all make mistakes and need a time to repent. But what about forgiveness? Does that not have a place in the new order of things? Or do we just "nuke 'em all, and let God sort them out."

Table 4 Core Belief 1 - Self-Image

Core Belief 1	
SELF-IMAGE: I am basically a bad, unworthy person.	
Interior World	Addicts conclude from their family experiences that they are not worthwhile persons. Feelings of inadequacy and failure predominate. Addicts often see humiliation and degradation as justified or deserved. Their desperate struggle with sexual compulsivity absolutely confirms this belief and enhances feelings of low self-worth. Addicts are committed to hiding the secret reality of their addiction at all costs, because of their unworthiness. And yet, the addiction guides almost all their behavior and decisions.
Exterior World	Addicts create a front of normalcy to hide their sense of inadequacy. They may even appear grandiose and full of exaggerated self-importance. As consequences to behavior emerge, the front contrasts with actions that seem to be degrading and self-defeating. Others see decisions or behaviors as irrational, incomprehensible, or self-destructive, but not normal.
Family and Friends	Close friends and family members become angry and frustrated with the addict's egocentricity, especially when there is insensitivity to others. Not knowing the interior world of an addict, they are troubled by what looks like destructive or strange behavior that does not fit the addict's projected image.

Table 5 Core Belief 2 - Relationships

Core Belief 2 RELATIONSHIPS: No one would love me as I am.	
Interior World	Addicts believe that everyone would abandon them if the truth were known. They have a constant fear of being dependent on others. Addicts perceive their sexual behavior as so bad that everything becomes their fault. Addicts assume responsibility for all the pain in loved ones. Honest guilt and remorse cannot be expressed because that would require honesty about their behavior. Addicts become progressively more isolated.
Exterior World	Addicts create an image of being in charge of life and in no need of help. They appear unaffected by any problem, but will often do extreme or indulgent things, as if making up for something. No explanation is offered, however. Some addicts may continue to be charming and sociable, but all addicts become unreachable personally as they close off all avenues of vulnerability.
Family and Friends	Significant persons in the addict's life start to feel pushed away, useless, neglected, and unnecessary. They become confused at seemingly generous gestures made in the absence of any personal warmth or presence. Anger and hurt accumulate with a sense of abandonment in reaction to the addict's irresponsible behavior.

Table 6 Core Belief 3 - Needs

	Core Belief 3
	NEEDS: My needs are never going to be met if I have to depend on others.
Interior World	Addicts feel unloved and unlovable, which means that other people cannot be depended on to love them, so their needs will not be met. The resulting rage becomes internalized as depression, resentment, self-pity, and even suicidal feelings. Because they have no confidence in others' love, addicts become calculating, strategizing, manipulative, and ruthless. Rules and laws are made for people who are lovable; those who are unlovable survive in other ways.
Exterior World	Addicts' rage about unmet needs in the past prevents the possibility of expressing needs now because they anticipate being rejected. Addicts appear no to want or need anything. They are purposely unclear about their intentions in relationships and are thus seductive in behavior. Specifically, they try to be affirmed or cared for without expressing what they need to, so they will not risk rejection. Addicts make extensive efforts to show how respectable and law-abiding they are.
Family and Friends	Those who are close start to see the double life, the Jekyll and Hyde. The addicts' ups and downs remain difficult to understand. Worse, distrust and disbelief in the addict begins. Things appear to be smooth, but the suspicion is there that they are not. Inconsistencies between the addict's public life and private life confirm these intuitions.

Table 7 Core Belief 4 - Sexuality

Core Belief 4	
SEXUALITY: Sex is my most important need.	
Interior World	Addicts confuse nurturing and sex. Support, care, affirmation, and love are all sexualized. Absolute terror of life without sex combines with feelings of unworthiness for such intense sexual desires. Sexual activity never meets the need for love and caring, but continues to be seen as the only avenue to do so. Addicts have a high need to control all situations in an effort to guarantee sex. Yet there is a secret fear of being sexually out of control. Addicts promise themselves to stop or limit sexual behavior, because of this fear.
Exterior World	Sexual obsession pervades lifestyle and behavior. Addicts make maximum effort to insure all possible sexual opportunities. Addicts at all levels of addictive behavior feel the need to control sexual access. That is, addicts involved in prostitution, exhibitionism, voyeurism, incest, etc. have in common the goal of protecting the source of supply. Seeking degrading or humiliating sexual experiences simply extends internal feelings of unworthiness. Addicts publicly profess extreme sexual propriety, however, even to the extent of moral self-righteousness about sexual matters. Cover-ups, lies, and deceptions are made to conceal personal sexual behavior.
Family and Friends	The addicts' protestations of high sexual morality obscure the impact of sexual impact on friends and relatives. Close friends and family members tend to reject suspicions of sexual compulsivity because of addicts' "values." As evidence of powerlessness over behavior and unmanageability mount, these persons become confused, not knowing what to believe. In addition, they do not wish to intervene in something so personal. Since they don't feel close enough to become involved, they choose the other option, which is to withdraw.

Table 8 Twelve Steps

	The Twelve Steps of Alcoholics Anonymous Adapted for Sexual Addicts
1.	We admitted we were powerless over our sexual addiction—that our lives had become unmanageable.
2.	We came to believe that a Power greater than ourselves could restore us to sanity.
3.	We made a decision to turn our will and our lives over to the care of God as we understood Him.
4.	We and a searching and fearless moral inventory of ourselves.
5.	We admitted to God, to ourselves, and to another human being the exact nature of our wrongs.
6.	We were entirely ready to have God remove all these defects of character.
7.	We humbly asked Him to remove our shortcomings.
8.	We made a list of all persons we had harmed and became willing to make amends to them all.
9.	We made direct amends to such people whenever possible, except when to do so would injure them or others.
10.	We continued to take personal inventory, and when we were wrong, we promptly admitted it.
11.	We sought through prayer and meditation to improve our conscious contact with God as we understood Him, praying only for knowledge of His will for us and the power to carry that will out.
12.	Having had a spiritual awakening as the result of these steps, we tried to carry this message to others and to practice these principles in all our affairs.

Table 9 Provisions for Addicts & Co-Addicts

Provisions for both Addicts and Co-Addicts		
Old Core Beliefs	Steps 1, 2, 3	The Program provides the understanding that each member is basically a good person. All learn to separate themselves as individuals from their addictions, which (as powerful illness) are destroying their lives. By admitting the addiction's power, hope emerges from connecting with others and with a Higher Power.
	Steps 4, 5, 8, 9	The fellowship of the Program surrounds participants with people who have suffered in the same way. They no longer feel unique. They trust and are trusted with personal secrets. They have the opportunity to assess their strengths and weaknesses, as well as to take stock of their own values and behavior. Their new vulnerability allows them the hope of depending on others outside the Program. They rediscover the fundamental human processes for restoring relationships through amends and forgiveness.
NOTE: Steps correspond to Twelve Steps of Alcoholics Anonymous adapted for sexual addicts.		

Table 10 Key Steps

Key Steps	New Beliefs	Integrated World
Steps 1, 2, 3	I am a worthwhile person deserving of pride.	Addicts and co-addicts have a new sense of pride. Power of the secret world is broken. Identity and integrity return. They no longer need to hide and can become open to each other and to others.
Steps 4, 5, 8, 9	I am loved and accepted by people who know me as I am.	Addicts and co-addicts develop a realistic sense of their strengths and weaknesses, of their personal self-worth, and of the limits to their impact on others. They take a new responsibility for their behavior, and their behavior becomes more congruent with their values. They learn that mistakes can be accepted, amends made, and forgiveness received. Addicts and co-addicts can become responsive and responsible members of the human community.
NOTE: Steps correspond to Twelve Steps of Alcoholics Anonymous adapted for sexual addicts.		

Sexual Addiction, Sexual Compulsivity, Sexual Impulsivity, or What?

Increasing attention is being paid to sexual behavior that is in some way out of control. Much of the recent literature has employed two currently fashionable concepts: compulsive sexual behavior and sexual addiction. At this time both concepts are of uncertain scientific value. Barth and Kinder (1987) argued for the use of *impulse-control disorder* as a description, which, in contrast with the *compulsivity* and *addiction* labels, is consistent with DSM criteria, but which has little explanatory value beyond inferring a problem of self-control. In the past other labels such as *nymphomania*, *satyriasis*, and *hyper-sexuality* have been used. (Rinehart and McCabe, 1997)

Looking at psychological or emotional behavior that leads to precursors of the action, which then lead toward criminal acts, is crucial in determining an effective path toward successful correction of the behavior.

A crucial issue that has received little attention is the extent to which out-of-control sexual behavior can be understood as a behavioral pattern at the extreme of the normal range, or rather a behavior pattern that is qualitatively different from the norm in ways that are problematic. (See Orford, 1978, for earlier discussion of this issue.)

The literature sexual compulsivity and sexual addiction has been preoccupied with issues of definition, particularly pertaining to DSM-IV, and has paid very little attention to possible causal explanations for why, in such cases, sexual behavior becomes problematic. Researchers often make statements about likely mechanisms (e.g. anxiety reduction or mood regulation), but these are more often based on clinical impression than on reported data. This discrepancy led Gold and Heffner (1998) to title their review paper "Sexual Addictions: Many Conceptions, Minimal Data." I disagree that DSM actually gives the true nature of sexual behavior. DSM may be used to determine some aspects of the disorder, but there is little that will guide the patient toward new thinking and new behavior.

Of the Few data-based studies to date, three have examined potentially relevant co-morbidity. Qualand (1985) compared 30 gay men presenting for treatment for compulsive sexual behavior with an age-matched group of 24 gay men who were presenting for treatment of non-sexual problems. While he found differences in their pattern of sexual behavior, (e.g. number of sexual partners and duration of sexual relationships), he found no group differences in mood or personality disorder. Raviv (1993) found the 32 self-identified sex addicts had higher mean scores than 38 controls on Symptom Checklist-90-R (SCL-90-R) scales for anxiety, depression, obsessive-compulsiveness, and interpersonal sensitivity. In an uncontrolled study of 37 subjects with self-defined "out-of-control" sexual behavior, Black, Kehrberg, Flumerfelt, and Schlosser (1997) found a high prevalence of co-morbidity with psychiatric conditions, most notably lifetime histories of substance-use disorders (64%), anxiety disorders (50%), and mood disorders (39%).

Researchers are paying more attention to the fact that out-of-control behavior can be reduced with mood-elevating drugs, such as the SSRIs (Fedoroff, 1993; Kafka, 2000; Stein, 1992). As yet, researchers do not know the extent to which such pharmacological benefits, when and if they occur, result from improvement in mood or specific inhibition of sexual response or both.

The best review of the literature in terms of theoretical modes is by Goodman (1997); we consider some of his conclusions further in this discussion. However, few of these theoretical ideas have been formulated in ways suitable for testing. In this project we explored the relevance of a new theoretical model to out-of-control sexual behavior, testing some preliminary hypotheses with a small study of self-defined sex addicts. We followed this with a more-detailed discussion of the theoretical possibilities and some further development of our own eminently testable theoretical ideas, particularly relating to the impact of negative mood.

If we assume that anxiety reduction or mood improvement is a key factor in many cases of out-of-control sexual behavior, we need to reconcile this with the conventional wisdom that most people experience a decline in sexual interest and/or responsiveness in negative mood states (Araujo, Mohr, & McKinley, 2003; Beck, 1967; Cassidy, Flanagan, Spellman, & Cohen, 1957; Kennedy, Dickens, Eisfeld, & Bagby, 1999). In addition, we must ask why such behavioral patterns persist and even worsen if the mood-enhancing effects are not transient but have such negative consequences.

Some evidence exists that the relationship between negative mood and sexuality is paradoxical in some individuals, with increased sexual interest occurring in association with negative mood (Angst, 1998; Mathew & Weinman, 1982; Nofzinger et al., 1993). We have been studying this relationship at the Kinsey Institute using a simple trait measure, the Mood and Sexuality Questionnaire (MSQ), which asks respondents to rate on a bipolar scale what typically happens to (a) their sexual interest and (b) their sexual responsiveness when they are depressed or experiencing anxiety. We have reported our findings for 919 heterosexual men (Bancroft, Janssen, Strong, Carnes, et al., 2003a) and 662 gay men (Bancroft, Janssen, Strong, & Vukadinovic, 2003). Whereas the majority in both samples reported a decrease in sexual interest when depressed or anxious, a minority (15-25%) reported an increase, somewhat higher with anxiety than with depression. Qualitative date from these two studies indicate a more-complex relationship between depression and sexuality than between anxiety and sexuality. Thus, increased sexual interest when depressed can indicate increased desire for sex or the need for personal contact or validation by another person. Conversely, those with negative association between depression and sexual interest may experience a simple reduction in sexual interest or a mood-related need to avoid personal contact because of low self-esteem. With anxiety the typical patterns are either preoccupation with the cause of the anxiety or stress, so sex goes "out of mind," or sex emerges as a means for achieving at least transient reduction of anxiety following orgasm. The idea that some individuals may be more likely to pursue sexual interaction or stimulation or become more sexually aroused when in a negative mood state, is of considerable potential relevance to understanding out-of-control patterns of sexual behavior.

Our dual control model of sexual response (Bancroft, 1999; Bancroft & Janssen, 2000) postulates that the occurrence of sexual arousal depends on a balance between sexual excitation and inhibition of sexual response and that individuals vary in their propensity for both excitation and inhibition, with typical inhibition proneness being adaptive across species. That is, in threatening situations where attention needs to be focused on nonsexual coping, inhibition of sexual arousal reduces the likelihood of being sexually distracted. Janssen, Vorst, Finn, and Bancroft (2002a, b) developed a questionnaire to measure these propensities (SIS/SES). It contains three scales, one measuring excitation proneness (SES), and the other two inhibition proneness.

46

Based on the items making up each scale, Janssen et al. labeled the first inhibition factor (SIS1) "inhibition in response to threat of performance failure" and the second (SIS2) "inhibition in response to threat of performance consequences." Scores on these three scales show close to normal distributions in non-clinical samples of both men and women. This is consistent with the idea that middle-range scores in each case reflect adaptive response patterns, while more-extreme scores reflect maladaptive response patterns. Thus, high SIS1 scores have been shown to be strongly related to vulnerability to erectile dysfunction in men (Bancroft & Janssen, 2002) and low SIS2 scores to certain aspects of sexual risk-taking in both gay (Bancroft, Janssen, Strong, Carnes, et al., 2003b) and heterosexual (Bancroft et al., 2004) men.

Theoretical models have been used to explain the paradoxical increase of sexual interest in negative mood states. On the assumption that situations that normally induce negative moods inhibit sexual interest and arousal to allow maximum focus on the coping process, it is postulated that paradoxical increase in sexual interest in negative mood states requires unusually low levels of inhibition of sexual response (as measured by SIS2) and relatively high levels of sexual arousability (as measured by SES). In a study heterosexual men (Bancroft, Janssen, Strong, Carnes, et al., 2003a), support was demonstrated for this hypothesis with the SIS/SES measures, together with a trait measure of depression proneness (ZDPR) and anxiety proneness (STAI), accounting for 19% of the variance in MSQ scores. In a parallel study of gay men (Bancroft, Janssen, Strong, & Vukadinovic, 2003), they were only able to account for 4% of the variance in this way. They also postulated (Bancroft, Janssen, Strong, Carnes et al., 2003b) that the paradoxical effect of anxiety on sexuality could be an example of excitation transfer (Zillman, 1983), which occurs when arousal induced in association with anxiety becomes incorporated into response to sexual stimuli in those with low inhibition of sexual response.

Past studies have also found the dopamine system of the nucleus accumbens produces the rewarding and sometimes addictive effects of sex, food, and drug abuse. It is believed that the same reward pathways are likely stimulated during and following pair bond formation between male and female subjects. Although the process of pair bond formation results from the activity of two different neuro-chemicals in separate regions of the ventral forebrain in male and female brains, the OTR and V1aR systems of the brain appear to activate two separate nodes of the

47

same reward pathway to form and reinforce pair bonds.

In studies of high risk sexual behavior, they found some interesting contrasts between the predictive value of SIS2 (sexual inhibition due to threat of performance consequences) and of MSQ (relationship between negative mood and sexuality). In both straight and gay men, low SIS2 was predictive of non-use of condoms; That is, the persistence of sexual arousal in potentially risky interactions reduces the likelihood of using a condom. Our measure of sexual interest when depressed (MS-1) was predictive of the number of casual partners but not of condom use (Bancroft et al., 2004; Bancroft, Janssen, Strong, Carnes, et al., 2003a). In gay men, our measure of sexual interest in states of anxiety (MS-3) was more strongly predictive of masturbation frequency than of frequency of sexual activity with a partner (Bancroft, Janssen, Strong, & Vukadinovic, 2003).

This "state of anxiety" is a direct result of society's rejecting the lifestyle of the gay man as immoral and against the law of nature, which is a reality the gay community is fully aware of, yet choose to do nothing toward seeking a change in that lifestyle. The AIDS epidemic has fallen on the gay community from the 1980s until today and only appears in bi-sexual men and thereby infects the women who practice a form of casual sex. The truth is, 99% of heterosexual married men will never come in contact with HIV, and therefore have a much lower risk of anxiety.

High-risk sexual behavior overlaps with but is not the same as out-of-control sexual behavior. However, on the basis of these findings, we formulated the following hypotheses as relevant to out-of-control sexual behavior:

1) A tendency to increased sexual interest and responsiveness during negative mood states will be more common in men with out-of-control sexual behavior.

2) Increased sexual interest associated with anxiety will be principally associated with out-of-control masturbation.

3) Increased sexual interest associated with anxiety will be principally associated with out-of-control masturbation.

4) Increased sexual interest associate with depression will be associated with out-of-control interaction with sexual partners (e.g., increased number of sexual partners).

5) In general, out-of-control sexual behavior will be more likely in men with a combination of high SES and low SIS2, partly because of the paradoxical association between mood and sexuality and

partly because of a more-direct impact of high arousal and low inhibition on self-regulation.

In this project, we used a combination of interviews and questionnaires with a small sample of self-designated sex addicts to explore these theoretical possibilities, as well as other qualitative descriptions of the out-of-control sexual experience. We have also used an age-matched control group for evaluation of the questionnaire data.

Method

Participants

Following distribution of leaflets describing the research project to local Sex Addicts Anonymous (SSA) groups, twenty-two SSA members volunteered to be interviewed and complete questionnaires (twenty males and two females). Interviews were recorded and transcribed. Each volunteer signed an informed consent sheet and was paid thirty-five dollars ($35) for his or her participation. In addition, eleven self-defined sexual-addiction patients (all male) attending the Kinsey Institute Sexual Health Clinic were assessed in a similar fashion. These patients were asked to sign an informed consent sheet and were charged only half the usual clinic fee as compensation. We obtained approval for the study from the Indiana University Bloomington Human Subjects Committee.

To allow testing of our specific hypotheses with the questionnaire data from the male sample, we derived an age-matched sample from our two studies of mood and sexuality. First, we excluded those outside the age range of the sex-addicts group (22-66). Then we randomly selected a 50% sample from each orientation group.This produced the same mean age for the heterosexual men. The gay men were, however, younger, so we randomly deleted individual cases from the lower part of the age range until the same mean age was established. These two sub-samples—heterosexual, $n = 196$, 57.8%, and homosexual, $n = 143$, 42.2%—were then combined ($n = 339$).

Interviews

Issues covered in the research interviews included the type of behavior involved, the importance of novelty or specificity, the steps in a typical sequence, whether participants usually attempt to resist the urge to act out, their state of mind while acting out, the extent to which participants can exercise control over their behavior, how various mood states affect the acting-out behavior, and the extent to which they use acting out to improve mood. We also asked questions about whether the individual had been sexually abused as a child, whether religion was important, whether there was evidence of other types of addictive disorders, and whether there was a family history of addictive disorders. Similar questions were asked of the client patients. Volunteer interviews were audio recorded and transcribed. We then analyzed the content of the transcripts along with case notes from the clinic patients to identify presence or absence of the key variable reported in the paper.

Materials

All male participants completed the following two questionnaires:

The Mood and Sexuality Questionnaire (MSQ; Bancroft, Janssen, Strong, Carnes, et al., 2003a; Bancroft, Janssen, Strong; Vukadinovic, 2003) This instrument is a trait measure that asks respondents to indicate what typically happens to (a) sexual interest and (b) erectile responsiveness when they are depressed (MS-1 and MS-2) and when they are anxious or stressed (MS-3 and MS-4; e.g., "When you have felt depressed, what typically happens to your sexual interest/response?"). Each item is answered on a bipolar scale with 5 indicating no change, 1 marked reduction, and 9 marked increase. The range for each individual item is, therefore, 1 to 9, and for the same score (MS-total) of the four scales, 4 to 36 (Cronbach's [alpha] = .85). For each mood state, there is a box to check if the subject has never been depressed (or anxious) enough to find out. Subjects checking this box are excluded from analyses involving this variable. We report only MS-1 and MS-3 in this paper.

Sexual Inhibition/Sexual Excitation Scales (SIS/SES; Janssen et al., 2002a, b) This questionnaire, with 45 items, measures three factors: (a) propensity for sexual excitation (SES; range = 20-80); (b) propensity for sexual inhibition due to threat of performance failure (SIS1; range =14-56); (c) propensity for sexual inhibition due to the threat of performance consequences (SIS2; range = 11-44). The response for each item ranges from 1 = "strongly agree" to 4 = "strongly disagree." Cronbach alphas for the three scales are .88, .83, and .66, respectively. Scores on each of these scales are close to normally distributed in the approximately 2,500 men we have so far tested. The scales have good discriminate validity with only modest overlap with measure of global traits of behavior inhibition, harm avoidance, and reward responsivity.

The following questionnaire was completed by the SAA volunteers and all the age-matched controls, but not the clinic sex addicts:

Zemore Depression Proneness Rating (ZDPR; Zemore, Fischer, Garrett, & Miller, 1990) This is a trait measure of propensity for depression in terms of frequency and severity. We used the thirteen-item version. All questions begin, "Compared to most people you know…" Three of the questions conclude: (a) "…how often do you get depressed?"; (b) "…how long do your depressions last?"; and (c) "…how deeply depressed do you become?" Ten further questions ask how often the participant experiences a variety of depressive symptoms (e.g., feeling discouraged about the future, feeling guilty or unworthy). Each question is answered on a Likert-type scale from 1 (e.g., "much less") to 9 (e.g., "much more"), with 5 indicating "the same as others you know." The range of scores on this measure is, therefore, 13 to 117. Zemore et al. (1990) reported on the reliability and validity of the ZDPR. Factor analysis showed a single factor structure accounting for 44% of the variance with a Cronback alpha coefficient of .90.

Results

Two SSA volunteers described behavioral patterns (one pedophilic, aged 47; the other exhibitionist, age 38) that were not described as out-of-control but rather as behaviors they would want to do if they could "get away with it." Both of these men obtained some benefit from regarding themselves as sex addicts, but as they did not report out-of-control sexual behavior, they were not included in further analyses. This left 29 men, mean age 40.1 years and two women, ages 38 and 41 years.

Behavioral Patterns: Twenty-two men were heterosexual, 1 bisexual, and 6 homosexual in orientation; both women were heterosexual. Ten men reported paraphilic behaviors (six involving children; five, voyeurism; and three, exhibitionism). Five of the gay men were "compulsive cruisers." Nineteen men and both women described "compulsive masturbation" as their principal form of acting out. One of the women told a story reminiscent of persistent sexual arousal disorder (Leiblum & Nathan, 2001), describing herself masturbating as "like a gerbil on a wheel."

The Relevance of Mood: Of the 31 subjects, only four men stated that their sexual acting out was not predictably affected by their mood. Seventeen subjects reported being more likely to sexually act out when depressed, and nineteen reported this in relation to anxiety or stress. Eleven subjects (nine men and both women) reported an increase in acting out in states of both depression and anxiety. Two men said they were less likely to act out when depressed; no one said this in relationship to anxiety. There was no apparent difference between those reporting increased acting out when depressed and those reporting it when anxious in terms of types of behaviors involved.

Resistance to Acting Out: Subjects were asked whether they found themselves trying to resist the urge to act out or whether at the time it was something they genuinely wanted to do. Eleven men and one of the women indicated that they tried to resist, but most of them did not give a convincing description of resistance. One man, for example, said, "sometimes I've wanted to, sometimes I've fought it, and sometimes I've done it without thinking." Another gay man with compulsive cruising said, "I tell myself not to do it, but I do it anyway." He went on to say that he devises tactics to avoid cruising and then forgets them. Another man, when asked to explain how he resisted, said, "I want to do it, yet I know it's unhealthy for me." The two most-convincing accounts of resistance were from men with obsessive-compulsive personalities. In both cases the sexual acting out was masturbation. In one case, the participant had intrusive thoughts about teenage boys or a compulsion to look at pictures of them. This led to considerable guilt and resistance, and he obtained a very transient calming effect by masturbating, followed by renewed guilt and depression. It should be noted here that the resistance was to the intrusive thoughts about the boys rather than the masturbation. The other man described preoccupation with sexual thoughts, which would lead to masturbation, followed by the need to take a shower, because of the "dirtiness" of the act.

State of Mind During Sexual Acting Out: Thirteen men and one woman described a typical state of mind suggestive of some degree of dissociation. The following are illustrative descriptions, each from a different subject:

> "…just find myself doing it…another voice in my head."
> "…an overpowering drive…nothing else is under consideration."
> "…numb, completely zoning out, not present, but conscious of reality."
> "…trancelike…there seems to be a chemical or hormonal difference in me."
> "…eyes glazed, numbing…unfeeling…focusing on the pleasure."
> "…trancelike state…kills time and pain…numb like a dream."
> "I am not aware of anything else…I block everything out…my preoccupation."
> "When I am sexually aroused, I click out."
> "…suspension of reality—nothing else enters your mind."
> "…like being taken over—a different person—trancelike, peaceful."
> "…feel detached from what is happening."
> "…like euphoria—like cocaine."
> "I shut myself off to everything, and I am oblivious of what I am doing."
> "…like a drug to numb out."

Other Addictive patterns: Ten subjects reported other addictive patterns either currently or in the past: three with drugs, four with alcohol, and three with both drugs and alcohol. One man described overeating; another, addiction to computer games; and one of the women described shopping sprees. Fifteen subjects, four of them with their own addiction histories, reported addiction problems in the family.

Questionnaire Data in Male Subjects

Comparison of our for the male sex addicts and for the controls is shown in Table 11. The sex addicts reported significantly higher MS-1 (sexual interest when depressed) and MS-3 (sexual interest when anxious) scores than did the controls ($p < .001$ in each case). They also had higher SES (sexual excitation) scores ($p = .029$), but did not differ from controls in either SIS1 (inhibition due to threat of performance failure) or SIS2 (inhibition due to threat of performance consequences). The subset who completed the ZDPR (our trait measure for depression) scored significantly higher on this measure than did the controls ($p = .02$).

Table 11 Comparison of Sex Addicts & Controls

Comparison of Male "Sex Addicts" and Controls						
Sex Addicts			Controls			
Trait	M	(SE)	N	M	(SE)n	p
MS-1	6.2	(0.41)	26	3.8	(0.11)243	<0.001
MS-3	6.7	(0.35)	27	4.3	(0.11)282	<0.001
SES	59.4	(1.17)	29	55.9	(0.45)338	0.029
SIS1	28.1	(1.05)	29	28.9	(0.13)338	ns
SIS2	28.0	(0.96)	29	28.3	(0.24)335	ns
ZDPR	67.0	(5.66)	13	53.5	(1.08)	337
NOTE: MS-1 = sexual interest when depressed; MS-3 = sexual interest when anxious/stressed; SES = Sexual Excitation Scale; SIS1 = sexual inhibition due to threat of performance failure; SIS2 = sexual inhibition due to threat of performance consequences; ZDPR = Zemore Depression Proneness Rating						

We divided the male sex addicts into sub-groups on the basis of several potentially relevant behavioral markers and each pair with each other as well as with controls. Mood regulators. Those who reported increased acting out when depressed were compared with the rest and with controls on MS-1 MS-3 scores. We made a similar comparison with those reporting increased acting out when anxious. The sets of comparisons are shown in Tables 12 and 13.

Table 12 MSQ Scores for Depression Regulators vs. Rest & Controls

MSQ Scores in "Depression Regulators" Versus Rest and Controls[a]					
Regulators (n = 14)			Rest (n = 12)		
Trait	M	(SE)	M	(SE)	p
MS-1	7.2	(0.31)	5.0	(0.69)	1 vs. 2 = 0.007 1 vs. controls <0.001 2 vs. controls = 0.06
MS-3	7.3	(0.32)	6.0	(0.62)	1 vs. controls < 0.001 2 vs. controls = 0.009
(a) Values for controls are given in Table 11.					

There was substantial overlap between these two "mood-regulating" groups; however, the "depression regulators" were significantly higher than the rest for MS-1 scores. The "anxiety regulators" did not differ from the rest for either measure.

Table 13 MSQ Scores for Anxiety Regulators vs. Rest & Controls

MSQ Scores in "Anxiety Regulators" Versus Rest and Controls[a]					
Regulators (n = 14)			Rest (n = 13)		
Trait	M	(SE)	M	(SE)	p
MS-1	6.0	(0.51)	6.4	(0.68)	1, 2 vs. controls <0.001
MS-3	7.0	(0.41)	6.4	(0.57)	1, 2 vs. controls = 0.001
(a) Values for controls are given in Table 11.					

Compulsive masturbators: Those whose principal out-of-control behavior was masturbation (n = 17), either using the Internet or other visual material, were compared with those whose acting out involved other types of behavior (e.g., cruising, voyeurism; n = 9). These comparisons are shown in Table 14. It is noteworthy that both MS-1 and MS-3 scores were higher in the non-masturbators, although neither difference was significant. The only significant difference was for SIS2, which was lower in the non-masturbators (p = .03) and controls (p = .006).

Table 14 Comparison of Compulsive Masturbators with Rest & Controls

Comparison of "Compulsive Masturbators" with Rest and Controls[a]					
Masturbators (n = 17)			Rest (n = 9)		
Trait	M	(SE)	M	(SE)	p
MS-1	5.7	(0.57)	7.1	(0.35)	1, 2 vs. controls <0.001
MS-3	6.5	(0.49)	7.1	(0.36)	1, 2 vs. controls = 0.001
SES	58.9	(1.32)	60.3	(2.36)	all comparisons ns
SIS1	28.2	(1.43)	28.0	(1.50)	all comparisons ns
SIS2	29.5	(1.22)	25.1	(1.09)	1 vs. 2 = 0.03 2 vs. control = 0.07
(a) Values for controls are given in Table 11.					

History of Sexual Abuse as a Child: To explore the possibility that a history of child sexual abuse may have accounted for High MSQ scores, we compared those with such a history (n = 9) to those without (n = 17) and controls. None of the comparisons was significant.

Paraphilics versus non-paraphilics: This comparison is shown in Table 15. None of the comparisons of the two sub-groups was significant, although there was a trend for paraphilics to score higher on SES than controls (p = .06), a difference not found for non-paraphilics.

Table 15 Comparison of Paraphilics with Rest & Controls

Comparison of Paraphilic and Non-Paraphilic "Sex Addicts" and Controls[a]					
Parephilics (n = 9)			Non-Paraphilics (n = 19)		
Trait	M	(SE)	M	(SE)	p
MS-1	6.6	(0.56)	6.0	(0.56)	1, 2 vs. controls <0.001
MS-3	7.4	(0.33)	6.4	(0.48)	1, 2 vs. controls = 0.001
SES	61.9	(1.87)	58.0	(1.43)	1 vs. controls = 0.06
SIS1	30.0	(1.52)	27.1	(1.37)	all comparisons ns
SIS2	26.6	(1.30)	28.7	(1.28)	all comparisons ns
(a) Values for controls are given in Table 11.					

Dissociators: Those who described a dissociative mental state during acting out (n = 13) were compared to the rest (n = 16), and these comparisons are shown in Table 16. There were no significant differences between the two groups. However, the dissociators scored higher than controls on SES (p = .02).

Table 16 Comparison of Dissoiators with Rest & Controls

Comparison of "Dissociators" with Rest and Controls[a]					
Dissociatorss (n = 13)			Rest (n = 16)		
Trait	M	(SE)	M	(SE)	p
MS-1	6.2	(0.76)	6.2	(0.47)	1, 2 vs. controls <0.001
MS-3	6.7	(060)	6.7	(0.42)	1, 2 vs. controls = 0.001
SES	62.3	(1.86)	57.0	(1.25)	1 vs. controls = 0.016
SIS1	29.8	(1.61)	26.7	(1.33)	all comparisons ns
SIS2	27.5	(1.49)	28.4	(1.28)	all comparisons ns

(a) Values for controls are given in Table 11.

NOTE: A comparison of the heterosexual and gay sub-groups showed that there were some significant differences in our trait measures. The homosexual groups scored higher on SIS1 (30.2 vs. 27.9, p < .001), ZDPR (58.3 vs. 50.1, p < .001), MS-1 (4.1 vs. 3.6, p = .04), and MS-3 (4.6 vs. 4.1, p = .03).

Discussion: What Can We Learn from this Study?

This sample of self-defined sex addicts is too small to draw conclusions about etiology, but it does allow us to explore our theoretical ideas and develop them further. We discuss our four preliminary hypotheses first, followed by some other aspects of the results.

Hypotheses

Hypothesis 1—that a tendency toward increased sexual interest and responsiveness during negative mood states is more common in men with out-of-control sexual behavior—was strongly supported by both our questionnaire and interview data. The two sub-scales of the MSQ that we examined, MS-1 and MS-3, indicated that increased sexual interest in states of both depression and anxiety were characteristics of the sex-addict group. Even though our sample was small, the differences with the controls for both measures were highly significant. Furthermore, the sub-group who completed the ZDPR (the trait measure of depression) had significantly higher scores than the controls, indicating that in addition to displaying this paradoxical relationship between negative mood and sexual interest, they were also more prone to experiencing depression than were the controls. With the interview data, all but four of the twenty-nine men and both women reported an increased likelihood of acting out in states of either depression or anxiety or both.

Hypothesis 2—that in general, out-of-control sexual behavior is more likely in men with a combination of high SES and low SIS2—was partially supported. Overall, our sex addicts scored higher on SES than did our controls, but they did not differ on SIS2. There was an interesting exception to this pattern: The sex addicts who did not use masturbation as their principal form of acting out (a small group of nine men) fir our hypothetical profile in having significantly lower SIS2 than both the compulsive masturbators and the controls, as well as having relatively high SES.

We found little support for the idea that low inhibition, as measured by SIS2, is a prerequisite for excitation transfer and the conditioning of sexual arousal in states of negative mood. There are at least two interpretations that might protect our hypothesis from refutation, apart from the inadequate power of this small sample. First, low inhibition may only be relevant in some cases, with other mechanisms playing a crucial role in the remainder. Second, the questions making up our SIS2 scale may not be addressing the most-appropriate situations.

Apart from our preliminary hypotheses, there were other findings in this study worthy of comment:

➤ *Dissociation:* Fourteen of the thirty-one sex addicts (45%) described a state of mind during their acting out which could be regarded as a form of dissociation from reality. We had not anticipated this pattern, and therefore, did not include any appropriate trait measure of dissociative tendency. We also found no obvious association between this dissociative pattern and other aspects of the acting out (e.g., mood regulation, masturbation), nor any significant differences between the dissociators and the other participants on our various trait measures. It is possible that a dissociative tendency has an enabling effect on the establishment of out-of-control patterns of sexual behavior, reducing the self-regulatory component that would be expected in most people. We should also consider the possibility that this self-description may be reinforced through the culture of sex-addicts groups (e.g., SAA), providing a form of excuse, if not justification, for their inappropriate behavior. However, six of the fourteen dissociators had little or no experience in such groups. Future research should more systematically investigate this tendency (e.g., using the Dissociative Experience Scale or DES; Carlson & Putnam, 2000).

➤ *Obsessive-Compulsive Disorder:* The concept of compulsivity warrants consideration. A few studies have looked for evidence of obsessive-compulsive disorder (OCD) among sex addicts, usually finding a small minority in this category (e.g., Black et al., 1997, 15%; Shapira, Goldsmith, Keck, Khosia, & McElroy, 2000, 15%). The compulsivity approach to conceptualizing out-of-control sexual behavior is usually criticized because it conflicts with the DSM-IV, which excludes such behavior from the obsessive-compulsive category on the grounds that "the person usually derives pleasure from the activity and may wish to resist it only because of its deleterious consequences" (American Psychiatric Association, 2000, p. 422). Compulsive thoughts of the OCD type often do have sexual content, but they are typically accompanied by negative mood and no sexual arousal. We would anticipate that most people with obsessive-compulsive personalities and a propensity for mood disorders would experience a decline in sexual arousability during negative mood states, as is the case for most people. Warwick and Salkovskis (1990) described two men whose obsessive-compulsive symptoms included intrusive sexual thoughts accompanied by penile erection. The awareness of the erection intensified the anxiety, and hence, reinforced the process. Is it possible that occasionally there is a combination of obsessive-compulsive tendencies and a low propensity for inhibition and/or high propensity for excitation or sexual arousal, with an atypical sexualized type of compulsive behavioral pattern resulting? If so, one would expect to find evidence of other obsessive-compulsive phenomena in such individuals. In this study, we found two men with such personalities combined with what could be described as compulsive and sexually arousing behavior patterns. Both had high SES scores (69 and 63), but one SIS2 score was elevated (35) and the other normal (28). This pattern is clearly not relevant to the majority of individuals with out-of-control sexual behavior, but may be relevant to a minority. Future research should aim to assess this pattern more systematically, both in terms of the specific acting-out sequence and in other aspects of obsessive-compulsive personality.

Toward a Theoretical Model

Our data, together with our understanding of the literature, suggest that in striving to understand out-of-control sexual behavior, we should be expecting a range of etiological mechanisms associated with different behavioral patterns that share the two key features of addictive behavior as described by Goldman (1997): a recurrent failure to control the sexual behavior and continuation of the behavior in spite of harmful consequences. Goodman's integrated theoretical model has three principal components:
  a) impaired affect regulation,
  b) impaired behavioral inhibition, and
  c) aberrant function of the motivational reward system.

61

This provides a reasonable framework for our theoretical discussion.

The role of effect: We regard the role of effect to be important in most, if not all, cases of out-of-control sexual behavior. For most people whose capacity for sexual interest and response goes down in states of depression and anxiety, such mood-related mechanisms are not relevant, and indeed, this may explain why their sexual behavior is less likely to get out of control. We should be cautious, however, in interpreting the association between negative mood and sexual acting out as a form of mood regulation or the deliberate use of acting out to improve mood. In some circumstances, when sexual connection with another person is motivated by the need to make personal contact or the need for self-validation or improvement of self-esteem, mood improvement may be the driving force. However, an alternative pattern possibly relevant to much of sexual acting out is that the negative mood (i.e., anxiety) leads to sexual arousal by means of excitation transfer. Once sexual arousal is established, there will be an intrinsic drive toward sexual release through orgasm, which will have the incentive of transient pleasure and post-orgasmic calming. Such a sequence may then be reinforced and established by conditioning, with the individual learning to think sexual thoughts (or seek out sexual stimuli) when feeling such negative mood. This explanation is consistent with the fact that more often than not the individual knows in advance, as a result of experience, that the transient reward will be outweighed by the longer-term negative consequences. We would, therefore, move beyond a simple notion of the sexual behavior as a mood regulator to define three effect-related patterns, each of which requires a certain relationship between affect and sexuality. The possibility of such different patterns underlines the likely variability of etiological determinants in out-of-control sexual behavior.

1) Pattern 1 involves the capacity to retain one's sexual interest or responsiveness in states of depression, which allows the pursuit of sexual contact with another person to meet depression-related emotional needs. Such needs may include establishing personal contact through sex, feeling validated by another person, or enhancing one's self-esteem by feeling desired by another person.

2) Pattern 2 involves the use of sexual stimulation to distract one's attention from issues that when thought about induce negative mood. This assumes that negative effect is being kept at bay by distraction. As Baumeister and Heatherton (1996) put it, "the source of emotional distress is not present in the immediate

situation, but is highly available in memory (e.g., just after a major rejection or failure experience). Under such circumstances, people will seek to distract themselves to prevent themselves from thinking about the upsetting event" (p5).

3) Pattern 3 involves the tendency for sexual interest and arousability to be increased in negative mood states that are characterized by increased arousal, that is, states of anxiety or stress. This pattern, we are postulating, is based on an excitation-transfer mechanism made possible by a below-normal level of inhibition of sexual arousability in the face of threat or other situations that elicit anxiety or stress. Our non-clinical data indicate that this pattern is far from rare, but for most people so affected, it is not associated with out-of-control sexual behavior. Although we found no clear support for this hypothesis in our small sample of sex addicts, we would still postulate, on the basis of our much-larger non-clinical samples, that this pattern is most likely to be manifested in solitary or masturbatory patterns of behavior. In this pattern, we do not see the sexual behavior as primarily determined by mood regulation, but as resulting from sexual arousal, which becomes a conditioned response to certain types of high-arousal negative moods. Once the arousal has been transferred into sexual arousal, there is a strong intrinsic need to pursue sexual release through orgasm, which, once this is recognized as a recurring and out-of-control pattern, induces further negative mood.

An important qualification of these patterns is the possibility that in some individuals, depression can be associated with anxiety, allowing for a blending of patterns 1 and 3.

A key and as yet unanswered question is why some individuals have the capacity for these atypical and potentially problematic interactions between mood and sexuality. In our study of heterosexual men, we found a negative correlation between MSQ score and age, indicating that paradoxical patterns are more common in younger men and presumably change for most individuals as they get older. We did not find the association with age in our gay men. This may be because our gay sample covered a different age range or because gay men typically have a different developmental history regarding the relationship between mood and sexuality. Nevertheless, the potential negative association with age begs the question of when such an association becomes established. One obvious hypothesis, which remains to be adequately tested, is that the paradoxical mood-sexuality relationship is developed during childhood or early adolescence as a consequence of early experiences that combine sexual response with negative mood, such as child sexual abuse (CSA) or induced guilt about masturbation. We found no support for this in the current study; those with a history child sex abuse did not differ in their MSQ scores from those without such histories. But because this sample was very small and we performed only limited assessment of the childhood factors, these results cannot be regarded as definitive. A better test of this hypothesis would be to identify relatively large samples with and without the trait of increased sexuality in negative mood states and compare them on various aspects of their developmental histories, including CSA. Coleman (1986) has postulated that the predisposition to use substances or behaviors to alleviate emotional pain may reflect an "intimacy dysfunction," which could result from child sexual abuse or neglect. It would be surprising if an early established pattern of increased sexual arousal and interest in association with negative mood could become a barrier to the normal incorporation of one's sexuality into close, intimate sexual relationships. In our study of sexual risk-taking in heterosexual men (Bancroft et al., 2004), we found that men in monogamous relationships had lower MSQ scores.

Clearly, assessment of the relationship between mood and sexuality should be carded out in future studies of out-of-control sexual behavior. Our MSQ has the advantage of being brief, with, by now, a substantial amount of normative data from both men and women. However, this is a very simple trait measure, which does not pick up the complexities of the relationship between depression and sexuality, or the potential admixture of depression and anxiety. We are in the process of developing a more-sophisticated instrument for these purposes. But in addition, further research should not rely on cross-sectional studies, such as that reported here, but should also use prospective methodology, such as daily diaries.

The role of inhibition: Goodman's second theoretical concept (1997) is impaired behavioral inhibition. Inhibition of sexual response is, according to our theoretical model (Bancroft, 1999; Bancroft & Janssen, 2000), an adaptive mechanism across species, and we have developed a psychometrically well validated measure of the propensity for such a mechanism (Janssen et al., 2002a). The concept of low propensity for sexual inhibition has already proved useful in explaining some aspects of high-risk sexual behavior (Bancroft, Janssen, Strong, Carnes, et al., 2003b; Bancroft et al., 2004). It is also central to our theoretical model of out-of-control asexual behavior, both as mediator in the paradoxical relationship between negative mood and sexual arousability and as a factor enabling sexual responses in risky situations. However, we found partial support for our inhibition based hypothesis with our small sample of sex addicts, and mainly with those who did not use masturbation as their principal form of sexual acting out. As discussed above, we may be missing some of the key aspects of inhibition with our SIS/SES questionnaire, and should certainly be prepared to explore other inhibition-related situations with different questions.

The neurobiology and psychopharmacology of sexual inhibition is complex, with an array of mediators and neuromodulators involved (Bancroft, 1999). However, serotonin does appear to play a crucial role. Kafka (1997) has proposed that a dysregulation of central monoamine function underlies out of control sexual behavior, Goodman (1997) reminds us of the difficulties in locating complex effects within the central nervous system or particular neurotransmitters, and the case has been made for formulating "conceptual systems" in the brain, based on function rather than specific neurotransmitter mediation or anatomic location (Bancroft, 1999). There is a clear need for well-designed, controlled studies of selective serotonin reuptake inhibitor (SSRI) treatment for men and women with out of control sexual behavior, in which groups are carefully selected and matched for indicators of impaired inhibition as well as other behavioral characteristics.

While direct investigation of serotonergic mechanisms in the central nervous system is difficult in humans, development in the genetics of neurotransmitters offers a new and potentially informative approach for explaining individual differences. Do individuals who develop out of control patterns of sexual behavior have lower levels of serotonin transporter gene markers (Lesch et al., 1996)? Another new approach to the study of central inhibitory mechanisms is the use of brain imaging (e.g., Redoute et al., 2000; Stoleru et al., 1999), by which certain areas of the brain are shown to be deactivated during response to sexual stimuli with arousal. Brain imaging, particularly for the study of complex processes such as sexual arousal, is at an early stage of development, but there is considerable potential here for future research.

The motivational reward system. Goodman's (1997) third theoretical concept is aberrant function of the motivational reward system. So far, we have little to say about how reward and incentive mechanisms may help to explain out-of-control sexual behavior. However, we are open to the possibility that some changes in sensitivity of the incentive reward system may occur as part of the establishment of an out of control pattern, changes comparable to those associated with chronic use of addictive drugs (Robinson & Berridge, 1993) and that may be relevant to behavioral addictions of various kinds (Holden, 2001). Once again, such mechanisms are difficult to study in humans, but brain imaging offers possibilities for the future (e.g., Breiter, Aharon, Kahneman, Dale, & Shizgal, 2001). However, until we have further understanding of such mechanisms, we should regard the concept of sexual addiction as no more than an analogy that may have beneficial effects, at least for some individuals, in therapeutic programs.

Self-regulatory failure: In addition to Goodman's three components, general issues of behavioral regulation deserve attention. To what extent is out-of-control or unregulated sexual behavior similar to other out-of-control behaviors like binge eating or overspending? Baumeister and Heatherton (1996) provided a useful theoretical approach to failure of self-regulation, which they described as a multifaceted process that can break down in several different ways. They paid little attention to sexual behavior in this article, but their theoretical analysis is relevant in several respects. They described three ingredients of self-regulation: (a) standards, (b) monitoring, and (c) the operative phase of regulation. Standards are of interest for our study, in particular the dilemma of conflicting or incompatible standards, which can undermine regulation. For five of our male sex addicts, religion was very important. It is not difficult to see how, in such cases, the unquestionable moral unacceptability of most types of sexual behavior would conflict with one's sexual impulses to undermine any sensible pattern of regulated sexual behavior. Thus, an individual who believes masturbation is evil and who has strong impulses to masturbate using the Internet will be unable to see that a regulated pattern of masturbation can be a responsible way of dealing with one's sexual needs. Coleman (1986) proposed that highly restrictive attitudes about sexuality result in inability to conform, starting off the cycle of guilt, pain, and compulsivity. We would suggest that such mechanisms might be important in some cases.

Monitoring is clearly important to effective self-regulation, and Baumeister and Heatherton (1996) suggested that alcohol as well as fatigue and stress can impair normal monitoring. Sexual arousal may also have this effect, and we have examined this closely in heterosexual and gay men in relation to sexual risk management (Strong, Bancroft, Carnes, Davis, & Kennedy, 2003). On the other hand, our theoretical model discussed above proposes that inhibition of sexual arousal may be an adaptive mechanism that could facilitate self-regulation. If correct, this could set sexual behavior apart from other types of behavior requiring self-regulation. Nevertheless, the individual with low propensity for inhibition of sexual arousal will be faced with the same self-regulatory challenge posed by other behaviors, such as eating.

An important aspect of monitoring, discussed by Baumeister and Heatherton (1996), is transcendence or focusing one's awareness beyond the immediate situation so that more distal concerns or consequences are kept in mind. The dissociative tendency, discussed earlier, could be directly relevant to out of control behavior by undermining, if not eliminating, this transcendence.

These more-general aspects of self-regulation, about which a substantial literature exists (Baumeister, Heatherton, & Tice; 1994), deserve systematic attention in future research into out-of-control sexual behavior.

Treatment of Sexually Violent Predators

Texas SVP Act

On September 1, 1999, the governor of Texas signed Senate Bill 365, which established the first outpatient civil-commitment program for sex offenders in the United States. The state legislature found that a small but extremely dangerous group of sexually violent predators exists and that those predators have a behavioral abnormality that is *not amenable to traditional mental-illness treatment modalities and that makes these predators more likely to engage in repeated predatory acts of sexual violence.* The legislature deemed that a civil-commitment procedure for long-term supervision and treatment of sexually violent predators was necessary and in the interest of the state.

Council on Sex Offender Treatment

The Council on Sex Offender Treatment was tasked with the implementation and administration of the outpatient sexually violent predator (SVP) treatment program (Title 11, Health & Safety Code, Chapter 841). This outpatient program was chosen strictly due to fiscal constraints. The annual outpatient cost ranges between $30,000 and $37,000 per client. Inpatient SVP treatment in fifteen other states (AZ, CA, FL, IA, IL, KS, MA, MN, MO, ND, NJ, SC, VA, WA, and WI) costs between $80,000 and $125,000 per offender per year. The outpatient civil-commitment program targets sexually violent predators being released from prison who pose a serious risk to community safety or who are at high risk to reoffend.

Sexually violent predators are committed, not convicted. The civil commitment program is neither a criminal charge nor punitive. The intent of the law is to provide intensive outpatient rehabilitation and treatment to the sexually violent predator. Civil commitment is different from a criminal sentence in that a criminal sentence has a definite time frame. Civil commitment continues until it is determined that the person's behavioral abnormality has changed to the extent that the person is no longer likely to engage in a predatory act of sexual violence.

The Kansas Inpatient SVP Act (1994 Kan, Stat. Ann. 59-29a01 et seq.) has withstood the constitutional challenges and has validated identical laws in numerous other states. The U.S. Supreme Court in the Hendricks case (Kansas v. Hendricks 521 U.S. 346, 117 S. Ct2072 138 L. Ed. 2d 501, 1997) ruled that as long as a state's ancillary purpose is to treat the sex offender and his/her due-process rights were protected, the state may commit the sex offender for an indefinite period, as far as the U.S. Constitution is concerned. On May 20, 2005, in a landmark decision by the Texas Supreme Court (Re Commitment of Michael Fisher, No. 040112) upheld the Texas SVP Act as civil in nature and reversed a lower court's ruling regarding due process and Fifth Amendment violations, facial vagueness, and punitive nature.

The Texas Legislature defines a "sexually violent predator" as a person who is a repeat sexually violent offender and suffers from a behavioral abnormality that makes the person likely to engage in a predatory act of sexual violence. The Texas civil commitment statute requires a "behavioral abnormality," which means a congenital or acquired condition that, by affecting a person's emotional or volitional capacity, predisposes the person to commit a sexually violent offense, to the extent that the person becomes a menace to the health and safety of another person. A "predatory act" was defined as an act that is committed for the purpose of victimization and that is directed toward a strange, a person of casual acquaintance with whom no substantial relationship exists, or a person with whom a relationship has been established or promoted for the purpose of victimization. "Sexually motivated conduct" was defined as any conduct involving the intent to arouse or gratify the sexual desire of any person immediately before, during, or immediately after the commission of an offense. A "sexually violent offense" is defined as indecency with a child, sexual assault, aggravated sexual assault, aggravated kidnapping with intent, burglary with intent, sexually motivated capital murder or murder, any attempt, conspiracy, or solicitation of the latter, or any offense under the law of another state, federal law, or the Uniform Code of Military Justice that contains elements substantially similar. The outpatient treatment and supervision program begins upon the person's release from the Texas Department of Criminal Justice – Institutional Division, discharge from a state hospital, or upon conclusion of a trial.

The Council, as administrator of the outpatient SVP treatment program, is responsible for (but not limited to) the following:

> - Comprehensive case management supervision
> - Residential housing requirements (if applicable)
> - Intensive sex offender treatment (intake, testing, groups, individuals, family sessions, etc)
> - GPS tracking (24 hrs./day, 7 days/week)
> - Anti-androgen medication
> - Mandated polygraphs
> - Mandated penile plethysmographs
> - Biennial examinations
> - Restricted transportation
> - Substance abuse testing

Only licensed sex offender treatment providers (LSOTP) who contract with the Council may assess and provide treatment to the SVP. Sex offender treatment groups are offense-specific and limited to ten offenders. Self-help, drug intervention, or time-limited treatment is used only as an adjunct to more comprehensive treatment. Sexually violent predators subject to civil commitment attend group therapy twice a week and have two individual sessions per month. SVPs are mandated to take polygraphs regarding their instant offense, sexual history, maintenance, and monitoring. The penile plethysmographs are utilized to assess sexual arousal. Failure to comply with the order of commitment is third-degree felony, which may result in incarceration in the Texas Department of Criminal Justice – Institutional Division.

Society should understand that SVPs are not typical sex offenders. These individuals are *repeat sexually violent predators at extreme high risk to reoffend* and community safety takes precedence over all conflicting constraints.

"Once a sex offender, always a sex offender!" Let us all pray that that is not true. The list of SVPs grows daily. And no one seems to understand why. We need to pay close attention to the behaviors of this classification of offender and deal with each of them appropriately, with regard to their individualized treatment plans.

In Conclusion

While acknowledging the importance to both the individual and society of patterns of sexual behavior that are out of control and have problematic consequences, we think it likely that such patterns are varied in both their etiological determinants and how they are best treated. For that reason, we consider it to be premature to attempt some overriding definition relevant to clinical management until we have a better understanding of the various patterns and their likely determinants. The concepts of compulsivity and addiction may prove to have explanatory value in some cases, but are not helpful when used as general terms for this class of behavior problem. Until we have a better understanding of the subtypes, we prefer the general descriptive term *out of control* to describe sexual behavior that is unregulated for a variety of possible reasons. In the meantime, we have postulated some testable, clinically relevant hypotheses and have developed or identified a number of measures suitable for their testing.

Protecting and Saving Our Children

> *"I honestly believed that what was occurring between my father and me was what occurred between all fathers and daughters. I felt connected and special with my dad."*
> —*Carol, who was abused by her father for six years*
> *(Pg. 119,* No Secrets No Lies *by Robin D. Stone)*

Parenting is the most important calling you will ever have. You are charged with loving and nurturing a human being—a living, breathing entity who does not come with instructions (other than the Bible). I wasn't until I had my own son seven years ago—until I held him in my hands—that I fully appreciated how dependent children are on those who take care of them. And when it was time for me to return to work and leave my baby with a sitter, I was terrified. "How could I trust him with a stranger?" I agonized. I would call home several times a day, make surprise visits to pick up something I'd "forgotten," and spy on them regularly at the playground until I felt my son was secure.

What enormous faith we parents must have to put our children in someone else's charge. If that person is not a relative or family friend, we try to get a sense of their character through interviews and references. Rightly so, we carefully monitor their actions and interactions for even the slightest signs to confirm our worst fears.

So who will protect our children from sexual abuse? The adults in their lives must take responsibility. Many of us are clearly safety-conscious; we strap our kids in car seats and seat belts, we hold their hands when they cross the street.

What We Are Up Against Now

You can't spot abusers just by looking at them or by watching how they interact with children. They can be anybody; a relative, a neighbor, a community leader, a professional. They try to appear trustworthy. They are methodical, conniving, and relentless. They have no problem smiling in your face and can even have sex with you while they plot to get your kids.

They will work to convince children that they should be open to sexual advances or that they like being violated. As a part of their sickness, many cannot comprehend that their actions are harmful. Or that the rules and laws that govern the rest of society apply to them. Their focus is on their own need for emotional or sexual gratification.

The reality of Finkelhor's preconditions is that parents do not have the luxury of thinking that "this won't happen to my kid" or fearing that informing their children about sexual abuse will frighten or harm them is some way. For their own protection, children from a very young age need to know what the term *sexual abuse* means, what actions and behaviors constitute sexual abuse, and what they can and should do if someone tries to abuse them. Here we will explore good ways to inform children without scaring them.

When abuse is disclosed, parents can get caught up in blaming themselves or their child, and let blame and embarrassment keep them from acknowledging and responding in a way that protects and helps the child. For adults who have been abused themselves, discovering that a child has been victimized can be paralyzing because it conjures up the entire old trauma, along with its feelings of fear, self-blame, and helplessness. But how you respond to a child's disclosure of abuse can make all the difference in how the child begins to heal.

72

A sexually victimized child will go to great lengths to mask any signs of the source of her guilt and shame, even while she's displaying symptoms of abuse by "acting out." Often, out of obligation to the abuser, a child may help to keep the secret hidden. How does this happen? Children want to be loved and are eager to please, and abusers know how to take advantage of them.

Profiling the Sex Addict

Dr. Carnes, whose 1983 best-seller *Out of the Shadows* drew attention to the problem, says sex addicts usually have a recognizable psychological profile. For one thing, the vast majority are men; they outnumber women four to one, in fact. More than 80% have some other kind of addiction: to alcohol, to gambling, to drugs. "Cocaine is the drug of choice for sex addicts," says Dr. Carnes. They generally suffer from low self-esteem. And they almost invariably report having been abused as children. Sex addiction, in fact, may be one of the many long-range consequences of child abuse, tragedy on a slow fuse. Abused kids not only come to feel worthless, they also come to think humiliation and shame are a part of normal sexual expression.

How many sex addicts are there? Dr. Carne estimates there may be as many as 7 to 14 million in the United States alone, three to six per cent of the population. The most common form of addict, he says, is the person who flits from affair to affair and may occasionally visit prostitutes, porn shops, or blue movies. Although he or she feels ashamed and is secretive about such behavior, it continues even despite efforts to stop. "Second level" addicts are those whose behavior has escalated into things that could get them arrested and often involves a victim: exhibitionism, voyeurism, obscene phone calls. At its most extreme level, sex addiction can turn into the most heinous of crimes, like rape, incest or child molestation. How can you tell if your sexual urges have started to run out of control? Dr. Carnes suggests that you consider the following factors. If most of your answers to the pertinent questions are yes, there may be an element of unhealthy compulsion in your sexual behavior like:
  a) Feelings of despair: After sex, do you have feelings of shame, despair, and emptiness?
  b) Secrecy: Do you feel a need to keep your sexual behavior a

secret? Do you thrive on the thrill of leading a clandestine "double life"?

c) Abuse: Do you engage in sexual practices that are abusive or exploitative? Do you have sex with partners who are not completely willing?

d) Empty relationships: Do you have sex with partners whom you don't really even know, or worse, whom you don't even like?

e) Compromised values: Does your sexual behavior consistently violate your ethical values?

The goal of these programs, according to one recovering sex addict, is to regain control of our life by "finding your original, authentic sexuality" under the heavy clouds of shame and sickness. But it's not easy. Another ex-addict says recovering from alcoholism is "a walk on the beach" compared with overcoming the shame and degradation of sex addiction. Still, if you've got a problem, a self-help group may be your best hope.

The goal of any sex-offence program must be "no more victims." Another ex-addict reported that the first step toward this goal is recognizing there is a problem in a lifestyle. This is a major point of resistance for many.

> *"Choice is made on the basis of conditioning, which produces an inertia of values resistant to change."*
>
> *— Dr. Carl Sagan*

This is true for all lifestyles. *Resistance to change* of a sexual lifestyle is brought about by long experience with sexual addiction, or any addiction to drugs, alcohol, tobacco or any other habit that spins out of control. The desired change can never be coerced by others, it will always, and can only be, a goal set by the individual.

Of equal importance to motivation of the individual, and to the success of any program of this type, is the hope for forgiveness for his or her wrongs of the past; where hope has disappeared, so goes the hope of a new life. And with the loss of hope, depression sets in. With depression comes anger, with anger the offense cycle can, and often does, begin again. This effectively defeats the possibility of reaching the goal of no more victims.

Yet it is *still* up to the individual, who made the wrong choices in the past, to accept forgiveness for that past and begin to move forward toward a new life, with new thinking, and new desires. I make no apology for saying; there is no source of forgiveness greater than the teachings of the Bible. There can be found experiences from the past which closely parallel the experiences of modern man, with all the pain and suffering we bitterly complain about today. If we choose to ignore this Book, we will ignore the teachings and go on to build our own "bible" of information based solely on our own experience. Those who ignore the teachings of the past will only discover the same painful lessons to be learned again. This is why I have, and will always, use the teachings found in the Bible as a foundation upon which to "grow" a new person. If there is a better way, I have not found it. And believe me, I've looked!

References

American Psychiatric Association. (2000). *Diagnostic and statistical manual of mental disorders* (4th ed., text rev.). Washington, DC: Author.

Angst, J. (1998). Sexual problems in healthy and depressed persons. *International Clinical Psychopharmacology,* 13 (Suppl. 6), Sl-S4.

Araujo, A. B., Mohr, B. A., & McKinlay, J. B. (2003). *Changes in sexual function in older men: Longitudinal datafrom the Massachusetts Male Aging Study.* Manuscript in preparation.

Bancroft, J. (1999). Central inhibition of sexual response in the male: A theoretical perspective. *Neuroscience and Biobehavioral Reviews,* 23, 763-784.

Bancroft, J., & Janssen, E. (2000). The dual control model of male sexual response: A theoretical approach to centrally mediated erectile dysfunction. *Neuroscience and Biobehavioral Reviews,* 24,571-579.

Bancroft, J., Janssen, E., Carnes, L., Strong, D. A., Goodrich, D., & Long, J. S. (2004). Sexual activity and risk-taking in young heterosexual men: The relevance of sexual arousability, mood, and sensation seeking. *The Journal of Sex Research,* 41, 181-192.

Bancroft, J., Janssen, E., Strong, D., Carnes, L., Vukadinovic, Z., & Long, J. S. (2003a). The relation between mood and sexuality in heterosexual men. *Archives of Sexual Behavior,* 32, 217-230.

Bancroft, J., Janssen, E., Strong, D., Carnes, L., Vukadinovic, Z., & Long, J. S. (2003b). Sexual risk-taking in gay men: The relevance of sexual arousability, mood and sensation seeking. *Archives of Sexual Behavior,* 32, 555-572.

Bancroft, J., Janssen, E., Strong, D., & Vukadinovic, Z. (2003). The relation between mood and sexuality in gay men. *Archives of Sexual Behavior,* 32,231-242.

Barth, R. J., & Kinder, B. N. (1987). The mislabeling of sexual impulsivity. *Journal of Sex and Marital Therapy,* 13, 15-23.

Baumeister, R. F., & Heatherton, T. F. (1996). Self-regulation failure: An overview. *Psychological Inquiry,* 7(1), 1-15.

Baumeister, R. F., Heatherton, T. F., & Tice, D. M. (1994). *Losing control: How and why people fail at self-regulation.* San Diego, CA: Academic Press.

Beck, A. T. (1967). *Depression: Clinical, experimental and theoretical aspects.* London: Staples Press.

Black, D. W., Kehrberg, L. L. D., Flumerfelt, D. L., & Schlosser, S. S. (1997). Characteristics of 36 subjects reporting compulsive sexual behavior. *American Journal of Psychiatry,* 154(2), 243-249.

Breiter, H. C., Aharon, I., Kahneman, D., Dale, A., & Shizgal, P. (2001). Functional imaging of neural responses to expectancy and experience of monetary gains and losses. *Neuron,* 20, 619-639.

Carnes, Patrick, PhD. *Out of the Shadows, (1983)*

Cassidy, W. L., Flanagan, N. B., Spellman, M., & Cohen, M. E. (1957). Clinical observations in manic depressive disease. *Journal of the American Medical Association,* 164, 1535-1546.

Clinton, Tim (2005). *Caring for People God's Way.*

Coleman, E. (1986, July). Sexual compulsion vs. sexual addiction: The debate continues. *SIECUS Report,* 14, 7-11.

Fedoroff, J. P. (1993). Serotonergic drug treatment of deviant sexual interests. *Annals of Sex Research,* 6, 105-121.

Gold, S. N., & Heffner, C. L. (1998). Sexual addiction: Many conceptions, minimal data. *Clinical Psychology Review,* 18,367-381.

Janssen, E., Vorst, H., Finn, P., & Bancroft, J. (2002b). The Sexual Inhibition (SIS) and Sexual Excitation (SES) Scales: IL Predicting psycho-physiological response patterns. *The Journal of Sex Research,* 39, 127-132.

Kafka, M. P. (1997). A monoamine hypothesis for the patho-physiology of paraphilic disorders. *Archives of Sexual Behavior,* 26, 343-357.

Kennedy, S. H., Dickens, S. E., Eisfeld, B. S., & Bagby, R M. (1999). Sexual dysfunction before antidepressant therapy in major depression. *Journal of Affective Disorders,* 56, 201-208.

Laaser, Mark R, Dr. (1992, 1996, 2004). *Healing Wounds of Sexual Addicition.*

Leiblum, S. R, & Nathan, S. G. (2001). Persistent sexual arousal syndrome: A newly discovered pattern of female sexuality. *Journal of Sex & Marital Therapy, 27,* 365-380.

Mathew, R J., & Weinman, M. L. (1982). Sexual dysfunction in depression. *Archives of Sexual Behavior,* 11,323-328.

Nofzinger, E. A., Thase, M. E., Reynolds, C. F., III, Frank, E., Jennings, J. R, Garamoni, G. L., et al. (1993). Sexual function in depressed men: Assessment by self-report, behavioral, and nocturnal penile tumescence measures before and after treatment with cognitive behavior therapy. *Archives of General Psychiatry,* 50, 24-30.

Orford, 1. (1978). Hyper-sexuality: Implications for a theory of dependence. *British Journal of Addiction,* 73, 299-310.

Quadland, M. C. (1985). Compulsive sexual behavior: Definition of a problem and an approach to treatment. *Journal of Sex and Marital Therapy,* 11, 121-132.

Raviv, M. (1993). Personality characteristics of sexual addicts and pathological gamblers. *Journal of Gambling Studies,* 9, 17-30.

Redoute, J., Stoleru, S., Gregoire, M. C., Costes, N., Cinotti, L., Lavenne, F., et al. (2000). Brain processing of visual sexual stimuli in human males. *Human Brain Mapping,* 11, 162-177.

Rinehart, N. J., & McCabe, M. P. (1997). Hyper-sexuality: Psychopathology or normal variant of sexuality? *Sexual and Marital Therapy,* 12, 45-60.

Stone, Robin D. (2004). *No Secrets, No Lies*

Endnotes

i Patrick J. Carnes, Ph.D., C.A.S. is the Clinical Director of Sexual Disorder Services at The Meadows, an internationally recognized, private multiple addiction/disorder treatment and recovery facility in Wickenburg, Arizona, 60 miles northwest of Phoenix in Wickenburg, Arizona.

The educational and therapeutic services for sexual disorders available at The Meadows are built on the technology evolved through Dr. Carnes' landmark study of the recoveries of 1,000 sex addicts. This work, summaried in *Don't Call It Love,* has been described by *New Age Journal* as "the best book on the market about addiction and its costs and consequences."

Dr. Carnes' pioneering career work includes the design of the first inpatient facility for sexual addiction in the country at Golden Valley Health Center in Minnesota.

Dr. Carnes serves as Editor-In-Chief of *Sexual Addiction & Compulsivity: The Journal of Treatment and Prevention,* the official publication of the National Council of Sexual Addiction and Compulsivity, which provides clinicians with innovative strategies for intervention and treatment of this emerging critical health issue.

The Meadows provides services to adults who are suffering from diseases of chemical and alcohol dependency, eating disorders, sexual addiction, depressive disorders, post-traumatic stress disorder, compulsive-addictive behaviors, dependent personality lifestyles, and other psychiatric disorders.

Dr. Carnes is a nationally known speaker on addiction and recovery issues. He is the author of *Out of the Shadows: Understanding Sexual Addiction,* Revised Edition, 1992; *Contrary To Love: Helping the Sex Addict,* 1989; *A Gentle Path Through The Twelve Steps For All People In The Process Of Recovery,* Revised Edition, 1993; and *Don't Call It Love: Recovery From Sexual Addition,* 1991. His first book on family systems entitled *Understanding Us* is regarded as a classic in family education and is now in many foreign editions.

New Times suggested his later book, *Sexual Anorexia: Overcoming Sexual Self-Hatred* "will create a new wave of understanding about sexuality and the dynamics in intimate sexual relationships."

Dr. Carnes' latest book, *The Betrayal Bond: Breaking Free of Exploitive Relationships* is the subject of a national workshop tour. It provides the basis for answering the question, "Why do people, like Nicole Brown Simpson, stay in their relationships?" In his book, Dr. Carnes finds a core similarity between addiction disorders and betrayal bonding. Both are rooted in abandonment; those who would exploit us betray us into bonding with them. Additionally, he demonstrates how to untangle from the suffocating ties of the betrayal bonds. *The Betrayal Bond* is published by Health Communications, Inc., of Deerfield Beach, Florida and follows a tradition of extraordinary literature by Dr. Carnes.

Dr. Carnes is often sought for his expertise on the subjects of sexual addiction, sexual anorexia, and traumatic bonding by print and broadcast media. His list of interviews includes CBS 48 HOURS, The Oprah Winfrey Show, Tribune Newspapers, *20/20,* Sally Jesse Raphael, Maury Povich and Inside Edition, as well as numerous radio programs throughout the country.

Dr. Carnes received his Doctorate of Philosophy in counselor education and organizational development from the University of Minnesota. Dr. Carnes serves as a member of the board of directors for the National Council of Sexual Addiction and Compulsivity and the National Advisory Board of the American Academy of Health Care Providers in The Addictive Disorders. Additionally, he is the vice-chair of the Interfaith Sexual Trauma Institute (ISTI), a collaborative organization of fourteen denominations working on sexual trauma within a faith context.

Information on Dr. Carnes' workshop and conference schedule and other programs by The Meadows on self-defeating relationships, personal growth and recovery, and post-traumatic stress is available by calling toll-free **1-800-MEADOWS (632-3697).**

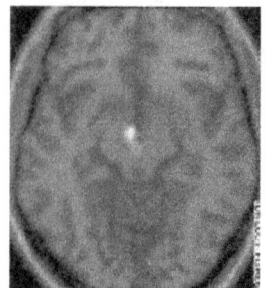

The brain of someone in love, looking at a photograph of significant other, shows activity in the ventral tegumental area.

By Elizabeth Cohen
CNN Medical Correspondent

Close your eyes for a minute and envision all the romantic parts of the human body: her beautiful eyes, his strong shoulders. We'll stop there, but you go right ahead and think about all the body parts you want. Bet you didn't think about the caudate and the ventral tegmental areas, did you?

These areas of the brain, while little known to most people, are helping scientists explain the physiological reasons behind why we feel what we feel when we fall in love. By studying MRI brain scans of people newly in love, scientists are learning a lot about the science of love: Why love is so powerful, and why being rejected is so horribly painful.

In a group of experiments, Dr. Lucy Brown, a professor in the department of neurology and neuroscience at the Albert Einstein College of Medicine in New York, and her colleagues did MRI brain scans on college students who were in the throes of new love. While being scanned, the students looked at a photo of their beloved. The scientists found that the caudate area of the brain, which is involved in cravings, became very active. Another area that lit up: the ventral tegmental, which produces dopamine, a powerful neurotransmitter that affects pleasure and motivation. Dr. Brown said scientists believe that when you fall in love, the ventral tegmental floods the caudate with dopamine. The caudate then sends signals for more dopamine. "The more dopamine you get, the more of a high you feel," Brown says. Or as her colleague, Dr. Helen Fisher put it: When you fall in love, "exactly the same system becomes active as when you take cocaine. You can feel intense elation when you're in love. You can feel intense elation when you're high on cocaine."

Is it love or is it sex?

Scientists then wondered: Does a brain in love look much like a sexually stimulated brain? After all, we associate love and sex and sometimes confuse them. The answer is: Brains in love and brains in lust don't look too much alike. In studies when researchers showed erotic photos to people as they underwent brain scans, they found activity in the hypothalamus and amygdala areas of the brain. The hypothalamus controls drives like hunger and thirst, and the amygdala handles arousal, among other things. In studies of people in love, "We didn't find activity in either," according to Dr. Fisher, an anthropologist and author of *Why We Love: the Nature and Chemistry of Romantic Love.* "We now have physiological data that suggests there are different brain systems for sex and love"

At some point the two do become linked. People in love have elevated levels of dopamine. Lots of dopamine, in turn, triggers the production of testosterone, which is responsible for the sex drive in both men and women. This helps explain why falling in love can make someone all of a sudden feel sexy. "Three weeks ago he was just another nice guy in the office and now everything about him is sexual," says Dr. Fisher.

All this research into sex and love got the researchers thinking. Most other mammals don't have this drive for romantic love and attachment. Why do humans have it? After all, we could easily propagate the species just with our sexual urges. Dr. Fisher thinks it has a lot to do with how difficult it once was to raise children. "Go back millions of years to the grasslands of Africa. A woman was carrying the equivalent of a 20-pound bowling ball in one arm and sticks and rocks in the other arm to protect herself in this dangerous environment. She needed a partner to help her. She couldn't do it alone."

And even today, when we have strollers and the environment isn't quite as dangerous, having a mate still helps. "There are women who raise a baby by themselves, but it's a lot harder," she says.

Male Brain – Female Brain

In their work with the love struck, the scientists found brain differences between men and women. "The men had quite a bit more activity in the brain region that integrates visual stimuli. This isn't surprising, considering that men support the porn industry, and women spend their lives trying to look good for men," says Dr. Fisher.

But she adds there's probably a more anthropological reason at work. Simply put: a man's evolutionary mission is to spread his seed. That won't work if he mates with an 80-year-old grandmother. "Men have to be able to size up a woman visually to see if she can bear babies."

The women's brain activities were a bit more puzzling. The scientists found that women in love had more activity than men in the areas of the brain that govern memories. Dr. Fisher theorizes that this is a female mechanism for mate choice. "There are no visual clues for whether a man is fertile, but if a woman really studies a man and remembers things about his behavior, she can try to determine whether he'd make a reliable mate and father. Thus, if it sometimes seems like a woman remembers everything—good and bad—about a man, "it's not just her being picky. It's an old Darwinian evolutionary strategy.

What's love got to do with it?

In the end, Drs. Fisher and Brown say what they learned from lovers' brains is that romantic love isn't really an emotion; it's a drive that's based deep within our brains, right alongside our urges to find food and water. "This helps explain why we do crazy things for love," says Dr. Brown. "Why did Edward VIII give up the throne for Wallis Simpson? The systems that are built into us to find food and water are the things that were also active when he renounced the throne of England."

Now their research is centered on the flip side of love. They've recruited college students who'd just been rejected by their sweethearts. Again, the scientists performed MRIs while these students looked at photos of the objects of their affection. This time the results were different, Dr Brown says. The insular cortex, the part of the brain that experiences physical pain, became very active. "People came out of that machine crying," she said. "We won't be doing that experiment again for a long time."

Elizabeth Cohen is a correspondent with CNN Medical News. Producer Amy Burkholder contributed this report.

---

iii "Hands down, the best darn book on masturbation!" —Journal of Sex Research, August, 2005, by Christina Clark

The Big Book of Masturbation from Angst to Zeal by Martha Cornog. San Francisco: Down There Press, 2003, 335 pages. Paperback, $22.00.

The Big Book of Masturbation from Angst to Zeal is an interesting, informative, and highly readable text that will be enjoyed by professionals and the general public alike. The entire book is excellent, yet there are several chapters that make this book a must-have for all who are interested in the subject. I will highlight them below.

Chapter 1, "Language, Meaning, and Words for Masturbation," has a very humorous and detailed glossary of both English and non-English phrases and words colloquially used as synonyms for masturbation. This section would be useful for educators who wanted to highlight the gender differences in the number of synonyms for male versus female masturbation, cultural differences in the number and quality of masturbation synonyms, and the apparent need we have to create such a large list of euphemisms for the act of masturbation.

Chapter 2, "Masturbation Through the Centuries," gives an overview of the history of masturbation from B.C.E. to contemporary time. It provides a concise overview of the belief systems that have shaped our current attitudes and understanding about the physical, mental, and moral implications of masturbatory behavior. This chapter might serve as a nice introduction to the topic for individuals who do not have time for, or interest in, doing extensive research on masturbation or as a brief introduction to the topic in a human sexuality course offered at the collegiate level.

Chapter 4, "Sociology: Who Masturbates, How They Do It, and What People Think," touches on some of the empirical research on masturbation.. Specifically, the author describes some research that speculates on the reasons why there may be gender differences in masturbatory behavior between and among males and females. This chapter is particularly interesting and would likely foster some lively classroom discussion about perceived appropriateness of masturbation for men, as opposed to the perceived appropriateness for women. Chapter 4 also has an interesting "how-to" section for professionals and the lay public seeking details regarding some of the myriad ways people actually go about the business of self-loving. This section might help reassure people that their technique, whatever it may be, is not strange or abnormal and that other people have devised creative ways to masturbate well. Clinicians may find this section useful as a resource for clients who may be experiencing guilt or shame associated with the perceived "abnormality" of their masturbatory behavior.

Chapter 5, "Anthropology: Masturbation Cross-Culturally," contains an interesting compilation of anthropological data about masturbation from different cultures and a variety of historical periods. Many of us who focus on the psychosocial facets of masturbation may not go outside our discipline to find information about masturbation. Cornog makes it easy to gain a multidisciplinary understanding of the subject from alternate perspectives.

Chapter 8, "Psychology and Psychiatry: Masturbation and Mental Health," is a particularly relevant chapter detailing the evolution of thought about masturbation in the mental-health community. This chapter also focuses on how the ideas of Freud, Stekel, Fenichel, and Ellis continue to influence contemporary beliefs about masturbation. It's also a useful read for students and interested non-professionals to help clarify why we have such a difficult legacy of "masturbation taboo" to overcome.

Chapter 9, "Law: Legal Codes, Regulation, and Masturbation," is a very enlightening chapter about the U.S. legal system and some of the state laws that effect masturbation indirectly via the control of the sale and use of sex toys and other devices that might be used for masturbatory purposes. The chapter details the six states that currently have "anti-sex toy laws" in place (GA, MS, OH, TX, VA, and AL) and the legal challenges these laws face. This chapter would most certainly spark lively discussion about the government's role in regulating sexuality and sexual expression.

Chapters 11 and 12 deal with the issue of masturbation and religion. These chapters are illustrative of the history of masturbation in Jewish, Christian, Islamic, Buddhist, and Hindu traditions. They also demonstrate the lack of consensus about masturbation within various religious traditions and the inconsistency in belief systems across time. These chapters also detail contemporary Christian teachings about masturbation and its role in relationships between men and women and in an individual's relationship with Christ.

The last section I would like to highlight is the section on masturbation and literature, which focuses on how masturbation is depicted in fictional works, poems, jokes, limericks, and other forms of creative literary expression. As a person trained in the behavioral sciences, I was unaware of the myriad references to masturbation that could be found in the humanities. It was as humorous as it was enlightening and would be an interesting alternative for educators looking for some unusual or infrequently referenced source to stimulate classroom discussion, or at the very least, a robust chuckle.

www.ingramcontent.com/pod-product-compliance
Lightning Source LLC
Chambersburg PA
CBHW081404280526
45788CB00009B/2985